SOCIAL MEDIA FOR REAL
■   ■   ■

Social Media In Marketing Communication

Copyright © 2012 Salih Seckin Sevinc

All rights reserved

Original Language: Turkish

Original title in Turkish: Pazarlama Iletisiminde Sosyal Medya © 2012

English Translation: Oytun Barlas

Createspace formatting by www.ebooklaunch.com

SOCIAL MEDIA FOR REAL
■   ■   ■

Social Media In Marketing Communication

Salih Seckin Sevinc

To Peyami Gurel

TABLE OF CONTENTS

Foreword 07

Preface 09

Introduction 13

Chapter 1: the change has begun 21

Chapter 2: content, sincerity and the first step 49

Chapter 3: the road map 149

Endnotes 163

FOREWORD

This part is important!

I want to thank you all; my parents who have named me after a writer without being aware of it; my wife Bahar who pandered to my whims during the process of writing this book and said "yes" to all my reasonable and unreasonable utterances; my one and only master Peyami Gurel who suggested that I should write this book; my puzzled brother Çagatay who kept on asking me "Well, where is it?" every time he saw me since the moment I told him that I am writing this book; my dear partners friends Mehmet Ali Altiparmak and Serdar Gencer who kept on working by turning a deaf ear to the absurd noises coming from my room at the office and supported me as they did in everything; dear Betul Becit who constantly sent me abusive tweets on Twitter in order to motivate me to finish the book; my college friend Didem Ulfer who appeared out of nowhere just as I was taking a break from writing and reminded me that finishing the book was the most important truth in my life without even knowing it; Burak Bulut Yildirim who said he should take some decent photos of mine since the book was coming out and did a phenomenal job with the photos; Tuba Cakir who contacted me and contributed to this book being printed from Optimist Kitap; Mutlu Dincer who contributed to the final state of this book in terms of design (I owe you all ice creams from Yasar Usta[1]) and my editor Utku Umut Bulsun who gained my admiration by answering me with

"What's the big deal? I read two books a day" when I said I added a few things while the book was in editorial process. Making of a book is a team work. You are great.

PREFACE

The making of this book is actually a social media miracle. I started writing the book during the summer of 2011 upon the suggestion of painter Peyami Gurel[2], my beloved teacher, but I couldn't start writing again after the long break (10 months) I gave myself due to my busy schedule. It almost seemed to me that the book was offended to me.

When I was mentioning that I have started to write a book on social media during meetings with friends, the first reactions in general were about whether I have already negotiated with a publisher or which channels would I use to sell the book. All our conversations had such an atmosphere as if the book was already written and published. But I had to do something before the processes of publishing or marketing the book can start: writing the book.

And this was the most challenging part. First, I had to finish the book by keeping the promise I made to myself. Of course the publisher was important and I wanted to work with a good one but first the content needed to be created. So I gave up on talking about the book around my friends and sector professionals. Sometimes, you have the illusion that you have already completed the job when you spell the words in your mind into words. And turning the words into a book could be more challenging due to continuous and rightful (from your own perspective) reasons (excuses).

My excuses were as follows: I can't find time from work, I can't get concentrated, I need to go far away and find a house there to write (writer mode), writing a book is about focusing, there is no time left from kids etc.

So, I gathered all my determination and will in April and May of 2012 and cleared up all my social media customers to whom I was giving consultancy services in order to complete the book. I directed the potential customers with whom I have been negotiating to other agencies as well. I told my business partners that I will be writing the book at the office and I won't be focusing on any other job during this time period. I spent all my working hours to write during June and July and only in this way I was able to finish this book.

When I felt I was coming to the end of the book, my heart was filled with excitement. Just as I was thinking that the time has come to start seeing publishing houses, I received the below e-mail from Tuba Cakir, media and communications editor of Optimist Kitap[3], through my personal page on About.me:

"Hello Mr. Salih, how are you? We read your article about Buyology, one of our 2011 publications, on your personal blog with admiration and we have also shared it via social media accounts of our publishing house. Brandwashed, the latest book of Lindstrom, has also been published by us in May 2012. We would like to send a copy to you if you would be so kind to give us your postal address. Sincerely yours, Tuba Cakir"

I replied with a thank you and shared my contact information. The next day Martin Lindstrom's Brandwashed was on my desk together with a kind thank you letter from Mutlu Dincer, the chief editor of Optimist Kitap. Of course I was happy about the book coming as a gift (Martin Lindstrom's Buyology has a very special place for me in all the books

I've read in the field of marketing) but I also couldn't help my eyes filling with tears. I thought that I have found the publisher for my book. The phone number of chief editor of Optimist Kitap was before me and the only thing I needed to do was to initiate a dialogue with her by saying "I wrote a book".

And I did precisely that.

See what kind of a surprise was prepared for me by a review I wrote on Martin Lindstrom's Buyology in June 2010 at my personal blog?

All the important questions such as how to get in contact with a publisher, how to talk, where to go, from where to start, how to explain were all answered through social media itself.

I suppose it won't be very appropriate to talk about how I felt during the process of the publication of the book for a business book. A book which has been built around social media was coming to a happy ending again through social media (from the perspective of the author). And this was leaving me with an unforgettable story.

The present book consists of three chapters in general: First chapter is about what the social media is, how the economy of social media works, what are its positive contributions to our life (just like the actualization of this book), how does it change our life and how is it differentiated from the conventional media understanding.

Second chapter consists of thoughts and examples on important social media instruments, the positions of these in the digital marketing communications, how to use these positions, liking/disliking craze and how to manage this craze ethically (how to increase likes in Facebook), how to use social media ads etc. In this chapter you will be informed about the social media strategy to be followed by using all the mentioned instruments and without getting lost in the social media craze. In other words, here, you will find inspired answers for your questions such as which social medium is appropriate for my brand, what does social media mean for my brand / corporation, what kind of strategies should I develop for my brand in social media, what is the use of social bookmarks etc.

And with the last chapter, you will end your reading with the influences of mobile devices on marketing communications in these days in which we are passing to mobile speed from computer (desktop) speed, which publications you should follow in order to stay up-to-date in digital communications, who is social media expert, the road map you should follow in social media, how to act without falling into the information trash and being contaminated by the blindness of change in this period in which the information is coming with the speed of light and without interruption, moreover the Higgs Boson (yes, you've heard it right, the Higgs Boson).

From the beginning, I wanted this book to be a book read with enjoyment rather than one with academic taste. Therefore, it is my priority for this book to teach new things and give enjoyment to whoever reads it, whether he or she is a social media genius or a newcomer with an interest in social media.

So read with pleasure. / Salih Seckin Sevinc @Temurah

INTRODUCTION

HOW DID I START HARBIYIYORUM?

I wrote my first article at Harbiyiyorum.com[4] in August 2009: "Why I eat and drink genuinely?"

There was a crisis. Istanbul Art House, the place I have been working at that time, was having a challenging time. The last thing people would be thinking about at those times was the paintings to put on their walls. The dire situation at work was absorbing my mind and it was quite exhausting to continuously try to find new expansions as a business developer and marketing expert.

I was going to go on a business trip to Naksan, one of the leading firms of Gaziantep[5] with which we had a business deal long time ago, with the hope of enabling new expansions again. But actually my subconscious was forcing me to make this trip to relieve my mind and enjoy while I am at it. The frame of the interview I was going to do was evident. The visit's details were clear. So, the only thing left to do for me was to make a research about what and where to eat there. The first thing that comes to mind when it comes to Gaziantep was obvious: Kebab.

So, the first thing I did was to lay my hands on Mehmet Yasin's[6] book, "Lezzet Duraklari - Taste Stops". But Mehmet

Yasin had written about almost every place but had skipped Antep. I immediately reached for my keyboard and googled "what and where to eat in Antep?"

The results I got were not going beyond subjective opinions of people written arbitrarily in many forums and the interesting thing was that not even one substantial article was found in the first three pages (I didn't go further) of Google. Think about it: I was tracing information fragments in the forum posts consisting of a few sentences when there must have been a whole body of work about the most important cuisine of Turkey. I gathered bits and pieces of information from websites and took notes. Meanwhile, something has begun to appear in my mind.

First, I thought that this was an insufficiency. Later, my will to write which I have been carrying along in myself for years started to get stronger. I started to think that maybe I could fill the gap in this area (food & beverage). First, there was a thing called "blog". The only obstacle standing in front of this could have been eliminated by actual research and writing. I didn't need a web designer. I didn't need a photographer. I didn't have any restrictions as to the style and length of my texts. I was able to share my articles with the world the moment I published them. There was no need for an agreement with a publisher for my articles to be read. All I needed was I and it was within me...

IN A WORLD WHERE EVERYTHING IS A LIE...

Yes, maybe I wasn't a gourmet columnist in a newspaper but I would have felt incomplete if I hadn't done this. Furthermore I loved eating. Back then, I knew that my biggest joy source and the most real thing was food in a world where everything was a lie.

Everything developed so naturally. My flight landed on Gaziantep at 9:30 p.m. I was at "Imam Çagdas"[7] at 10:30 p.m.

The first food destination when you go to Antep is Imam Cagdas. You can find all kinds of kebab here. You can also find comments on forums about this place's decency, rootedness and the taste of the food. But I had a theory in my mind that I have been entertaining for years waiting to surface: A place cannot cook all the dishes in their best. A place can only cook the best of one, or maximum two dishes and sticks in people's minds with these dishes.

Let me try to explain this in other words. For example, whenever we crave for meatballs, we go to "Ekpress Inegol Koftecisi"[8] as a family. If we are to have a tripe soup (yikes!), we go to "Cumhuriyet Iskembecisi"[9]...

Now let us direct this projection on brands. Does anything other than jean pants come to your mind when you hear Levi's? Or do you think of Cappy, for example, when somebody says Coca-Cola? Probably not.

Then, I tried to prove this theory to myself by asking locals in Gaziantep. Among all the kebab places, lahmacun (Turkish pizza) places, liver places, katmer (flaky pastry) and baklava places people were separating the most renowned or the best ones in their mind and were pointing at these. Local people from Antep were pointing at "Katmerci Zekeriya"[10] when katmer was in question. In other words, this meant: if you are going to eat "katmer" in Gaziantep, don't waste your time in other places and go directly to Katmerci Zekeriya.

GOING ON AS THE TASTE DETECTIVE

I wandered around just like a taste detective during the days I was in Antep. Of course I ate continuously. I pigged out on food. I tried everything. This trip was a fun period as much as it was hard on my stomach. I was chatting with people, taking photos of the places I've been and dishes

I've tasted, asking questions about the foods and enjoying it more and more by seeing how enthusiastic people were about sharing their knowledge. I have gained immense knowledge about Gaziantep culinary culture and the masters behind this culture during the trip I have made with a spirit of exploration.

When I returned home, I knew what and how to write in my blog. I would narrow down the area. My articles would be about only one region and only one dish made at a single place would be emphasized. The articles would have a specific content just like the search I had done in Google before going to Antep. In addition, I didn't have a clue back then about the concepts such as "Google Friendly", "SEO - Search Engine Optimization" or "Niche". (For the ones who don't know, little cells developed to better provide for the needs of a small consumer group is called "niche". For example, a website which only provides information about and sells "Chile Wines" is a niche site.) Later, all these concepts have been used for Harbiyiyorum website.

So the titles of my first articles were: "Where to eat lahmacun in Gaziantep?", "Where to eat baklava in Gaziantep?", "Where to eat katmer in Gaziantep?" etc.

I jumped to my keyboard immediately after returning from Antep. First I needed to name my project. Actually, everybody was living on food. But not everybody was competent in terms of taste or the meaning of the food they were eating. So we (meaning me and people like me) were not from the flock of regular eaters. We were eating "genuinely" (harbi). I immediately opened a blog named **Harbiyiyorum** on Blogger.com, a blog service bought by Google in 2003. And my motto was "Gourmet of the People" with the purpose of teasing the guys who were taking up all the high places and who had emptied the title of "Gourmet".

My first article in Harbiyiyorum.com named "Why I eat

and drink genuinely?" was published in August 2009. It began with the following sentence: "Since we saw everything became a lie in the times in which the end of the world is being experienced, we thought someone might as well tell the truth about food & beverage so that every person with a sense of taste could eat and drink properly."

You might have understood from the above text that I was fed up with the crisis and the puff appearance of business world at that time. Therefore, Harbiyiyorum was an escape at first. But I would recognize much later that this was a new expansion for me in the field of marketing communications.

So that's when everything started. Since then, I write articles on Harbiyiyorum.com with the same approach.

INSINCERE, HOLLOW MARKETING

While I was writing on Harbiyiyorum, interesting ideas about my job started to come to me in no time. Harbiyiyorum was a kind of therapy for me in a period in which I felt I had to continuously polish my marketing messages in order to put forth our products in a better way. I didn't have to sell anything to people here. I didn't have the obligation to write as people want me to write either. I was just writing as I like.

In my professional life, on the other hand, I was being abused by the one-sided, self-absorbed messages of the firms in which they were continuously trying to sell me things. Yet this was the rule of the game and I felt I needed to do the same most of the time myself. But this was both demoralizing and exhausting at the same time. All the marketing processes seemed so different from what I have been taught in college, as insincere and empty concepts towards the end of 2009.

Precisely one year later, Ahmet Ors[11] announced Harbiyiyorum.com among "The Best Food & Beverage Blogs of Turkey" in Lezzet Supplement of Sabah newspaper.[12] Yigal and Ansel, American journalists and the owners of IstanbulEats, started to use the articles in Harbiyiyorum.com and translated them to English. How could I have known that I was going to appear full page on Hurriyet's supplement Cumartesi when Savas Ozbey called me for an interview in February 2011? Harbiyiyorum.com today is a website still continuing with a blog approach with 27 thousand single visitors monthly and has reached 100 thousand hits in total, in just four years. Some of you might think "This is nothing to be proud of!" but as I write these sentences there are 120 articles on the website and I can also tell you that I write two articles every month as an average; maybe these datas might change your mind. The content people would know that this is a true success. Two added articles each months and increase in the visitor numbers everyday are significant indicators. Moreover, the interest from conventional media even from the first year is also a great achievement.

THE KEY TO SUCCESS IN INTERNET: CONTINUITY AND PATIENCE

Yes, maybe I may not be able to print a book with hundred articles in my hand yet. But if I had published a book first, Harbiyiyorum wouldn't have achieved such a success. And I know that Harbiyiyorum.com will continue to be successful more and more everyday as long as I keep on writing. Since success in Internet requires continuity and patience.

But what is the secret of the success of Harbiyiyorum? I will be sharing the factors lying behind this reality in the present book.

Of course the first step to success was to create a high quality and original content. But the processes starting with

Harbiyiyorum which have been unique experiences for me have deleted everything that I knew about marketing communications and recreated them.

I am writing this book to share the knowledge I gained starting from an unexpected project and directed me to deepen my studies in social media and also enabled me to give consultancy services and trainings for corporations. I suppose the real success comes from this; The will to share.

I am well aware that knowledge multiplies as it is shared.

CHAPTER 1

The Change has begun

AS A FAN OF MARKETING AND BUSINESS DEVELOPMENT, when I first started to think about the ways to use the successful development of Harbiyiyorum of which I had no clue at first, in my own business life, I found myself in a formation which had been already working in the field of social media and developing projects and applications in the field. Everything developed naturally. I wouldn't have been wise if I didn't enter into this "New Media" as a marketing professional.

The weirdest thing was that conventional media people were living in their stone castles very happily, not knowing much about this wind coming from another direction.

The good thing was that this process has formed itself through a social experience and it had a philosophical foundation. Yes, the economic crisis experienced in 2009 had become the driving force of social media. That's why I love crises. They initiate real fundamental changes. Like By-Pass or detox...

When we really hit the rock bottom, we start to internalize and understand what we really need with a forceful feeling and we start to surface with all this newly found illuminations. The best thing to do when we have faced ourselves after so much labor we had been giving is to be sincere towards our own existence. Only then, we start to pour out what was poisoning us and let the chips fall as they may.

All this becomes the herald of other new found things. Big crises always prepare a new foundation for new formations and changes, and do so in a very fast way.

That is how social media appeared most clearly before our eyes. In other words after this crisis, after the moments of depression...

Before social media drew the attention it has now, I was working in a bubble field (art business). Moreover this bubble was not only true for my own sector. I must say that the crisis originated from the real estate market (mortgage). Everything was being presented in a different way than it actually is, and the use of conventional media was being designed to rely on lies completely. The one-sided ads found on TVs, newspapers and magazines had already started to pester the life out of everybody. The main corners were taken and a significant income was being earned in the dull advertisement business. Brands were actually saying the same thing through all the fancy words and creative texts: "Buy my product because it is the best!"

The consumers, on the other hand, were already tired of being forced to buy things. A new credit card was being sent to your address when you already had two, or a bank was begging to you "please get a second health insurance from us. Please! Come on! Please!" when you were already paying for a private health insurance; new insurance companies were coming out of nowhere and trying to sell to you an incredible new health service for only 20 TL[13] and doing this by using sales pitches like "What is 20 TL? You are already spending that amount of money to trivial things"; in short we were facing hypocrites behind the lie of "We care about you" when what they actually were saying "We care about your money, not you" (we still encounter this kind of approaches but it is significantly diminishing if you look at it closely.)

CONVENTIONAL MEDIA HEADED FOR THE LAST ROUNDUP

Conventional media has been already headed for the last roundup and finally its bubble had burst. The change had already begun when the bubble had burst. People no more wanted to be sold things; they wanted to use their free will to satisfy their own wants suitable to their own nature and formed only according to their own needs. This condition could have only be met by the brands which presented themselves sincerely (not desperately trying to sell their products but only explain their benefits) by finding the communication channels enabling them to introduce themselves genuinely and creating a superior consumer experience.

Today, individuals look for information related to the real user experience from blogs, Facebook, wikis, dictionary forums and evaluate this information before they buy a product or a service. Moreover they share their own buying experiences on the web. Thus this content is not necessarily a content to trigger the sales. Internet shows for the first time what the right usage of Web 2.0 is. And of course, the entire world participates to this blast.

The information age led by the Internet experienced its second evolution with the concept of Web 2.0 introduced by O'Reilly Media towards the end of 2004. The process which started with the development in websites after the "dot com" madness of firms in the early 2000s (everybody started to buy domain names with .com extension during the early 2000s together with the formation of websites) and online shopping is completely designed on people's sharing of their own experiences. And which are the websites in which people are creating content? The first ones that come to my mind are Facebook, Youtube, Twitter, Blogs, Flickr, Linkedin, Foursquare, Pinterest...

I won't be talking much about what Web 2.0 is, since you can find satisfying answers if you search for it in the Internet.

To conclude, these kinds of services become more specific and detailed each passing day. We encounter with a Web 2.0 project or a mobile application of it for every mode and every need of human kind. Communities are coming together in these projects which are different in the area of interest and needs. These communities come to mean "Brand New Marketing Areas" for the marketing professionals. In other words, these are the other social media fields.

Yes. This new ship has not departed yet. It continues to collect its passengers from the docks. The people who can get their place in this ship before it leaves with the speed of light are really lucky people. Since later, neither 4P of marketing will be left nor will conventional media return to its old, glorious days.

Another truth is that we are heading towards an online future in which the sincere trade told by our parents like a tale, in other words "decent" trade and most important of all sincerity will prevail. This is a future in which solidarity, sharing, honesty will rule... and we will see all the communities, each becoming an online village and only the ones on the right track will be successful.

There will always be wrong-doers, not able to understand completely what's going on or just being evil-minded. But there is no escape from this mode of communication from now on.

What I try to say is, even if you are trying to express yourself in other ways with the habit you have formed through conventional media, other will already be tweeting the truth about you.

The carpet you have been sitting on for years will be pulled under you soon and very fast. Be prepared to be swept away with social media!

ECONOMY OF SOCIAL MEDIA AND CHANGE

We are at the very beginning of an era which is new and quite promising for organizations as well as consumers: Economy of social media.

Social media saves people from doing the same jobs over and over again. This saves you a lot of time to increase individual awareness or spend time with your loved ones. If a mother sees that fifteen of her closest friends have bought the same model of push-chair, she won't be spending too much time to make researches in order to buy one since this has already been done by her friends. This saves billions of research hours in total and transforms these hours into a meaningful and high quality time to be used for people's own needs.

From now on, winners won't be the ones who own the cornerstones in conventional media but the ones who can present their products and services through social media in the best way possible. And this actually indicates that the real winners would be consumers.

Well, where did this social media came from and became a phenomena in Internet in less then three years? Now even in TV ads we see brands directing people towards their social media addresses. The information transfer in social media which spread around as if a comet hit it, has become stunning when compared to its status 5 years ago. (But of course all kinds of scientific developments and technological improvements have the same head spinning speed, let's hope we'll be able to enjoy it.)

BROADCASTING TO THE RIGHT PERSON

All this could be said to cause information indigestion in people. Since status updates, micro blogs, social bookmarks, wikis, podcasts, video posts, photo sharing websites etc. enable more content production and increase in the dissemination of information compared to before. Together with such an increase in the quantity of information, we could as well say that confusion is more than likely and this is not very healthy for our sanity. But we can see that the matter is much different than it seems when we analyze it more in depth.

In conventional media, a broadcast is expected to reach millions of people without targeting the right audience group. On the other hand, the opposite of this which would mean millions of broadcasts reaching one right person, is not possible, all the contents found in a newspaper would not necessarily appeal to us. Some of us might like politics; the others might only be enjoying reading the articles about food. In this context, social media achieves the opposite of what conventional media achieved.

We want to see the broadcasts we like and contents that relate to us in printed media, on TV or Internet media. The websites that publish with a focus niche-buying people are able to gather people with the similar interests together and these websites offer us just the contents we need. In short, mass marketing has entered "Mass Marketing to Niches" era now.

For example, we gather just the information we want by searching in Google. This is a very relaxing thing for the human brain.

All of us want both to live our own individuality freely and to be in and getting accepted by a social circle. Human being is such a creature. This is what experts say.

Now, we keep diaries open to everybody in order to stay in touch with people since our strangest motive is to be accepted by society. The care shown for privacy diminishes as the generation gets younger. It is becoming more and more ordinary every passing day to make visible the things which in the old day were considered private. In other words, we have nothing to hide now.

Today, you don't even have to search for new in Internet. If a friend of mine considers some news or a video worth to be shared, that becomes automatically valuable for me as well.

Whenever we want to hear about some important news or watch our favorite show, we don't need to wait until the first day of the week or the reruns of the channel in question since that news is already within our reach in a synchronized way. In short, information comes to us by itself now.

"I AM IN SOCIAL MEDIA, THEREFORE I EXIST"

The main motive of people in their attempt to use social media is the desire to see and understand what others are doing. In other words curiosity!

Even just for this reason, I want conventional media to develop Web 2.0 compatible strategies in the coming days. TV broadcasts as well as newspapers should produce content parallel to web publications... Otherwise they will bleed out quickly and will need a respiratory equipment to survive. We clearly see that advertisement revenue in conventional media is being reduced quickly and people are running towards social media.

We see a change with a similar speed in "Resumes" as well. Four or five years ago the specifics of preparing a resume consisted of techniques of preparing cover letters, how to bring yourself to the fore etc., in other words how to tell about yourself in a fancy way in two pages in a one-sided manner, just as it was in conventional media. The most important things influencing a job application was resumes. Your almighty resume was your only mask to bring you the job you will be happy with, your only treasure to present you professionally to the employers. It was taking hours to prepare a successful one. Nowadays we are able to prepare professional resumes within minutes using simple mobile applications.

Nobody can deny that today, from the minute you open an account in your own name in social media, you are considered as having disclosed all your secrets and you have already begun to prepare the most transparent resume you can ever prepare in your life.

It is very simple; I and my partners immediately look for the Facebook account, what they have written on Twitter and LinkedIn profile whenever somebody sends us a resume. Since their existence in there is much more real than their two-page resume and projects the person in a more realistic way. It definitely gives much more information about the candidate than a simple resume. It projects the mirror reflection of the person exactly like themselves rather than their desire on how to appear to others.

If somebody has written on their classic resume that they have completed master's degree on marketing in United Kingdom but haven't written their social network information or if they do not exist on social media, then they have no chance in working with us. For the ones who don't know, we are a digital media agency. How could they stand a chance?

But let's say that the applicant is a photographer or a blog writer. They can show how creative they are in photography or how good copy writers they are by informing me about their Flickr or blog address. In this case we don't even need their resume. With this information, a photographer's employment in the related field is more likely than the situation in which they have indicated the master's degree they had in United Kingdom in their resume.

The classical .pdf and word resumes do not stand any

other chance than to be old documents to be archived in human resources departments of organizations. OK, maybe they are not that outdated but that resume you hold in your hand proudly does not differ from the ones belonging to the other five hundred people looking for employment in your city.

For now, social media shows your own real color. Now, your resume consists of the last message you've written on Twitter, your comment on Facebook, the article you've published in your blog, the music you've shared, the photo you've uploaded on Instagram, the videos you have favorited on Youtube...

If an executive is looking for somebody to employ and cannot decide between two candidates, the choice will depend on the link they think they have with the person in question. This link could be an article you wrote, a music you shared or you interest in fine arts. Persons who can present themselves correctly in social media would be taking the job.

EVERYONE HAS SOMETHING TO SAY ON SOCIAL MEDIA

There is a phrase marketing people love: WOMM, "Word of Mouth Marketing." Many books refer to it as "Buzz Marketing" as well. If we are to explain a little; you know how our purchasing behavior is always more effected by the recommendations of our acquaintances on the products they personally use... This is exactly it. Word of mouth or buzz, whatever it is called, is the most important weapon of a marketing expert.

I watched a beautiful movie of 2009 featuring Demi Moore emphasizing the dramatic aspects of WOMM: "The Joneses"[14] I recommend it to you, watch if you can.

You know how we used to want to have the same

Amiga computer the son of our neighbor Mrs. Green owned already. Or how we used to say our mother that the laundry of Mrs. Green smelled better and our mother used to ask Mrs. Green, which softener she uses and bought the same! That is WOMM.

And now social media enables us to practice the most effective marketing method, word of mouth in a global scale. In other words, everyone has something to say in social media. The mouths close to each other influence each other's purchasing behavior more effectively as they always have.

I hear some of you saying "But what do I care if my friend eats the most tasteful jam in the world? Or what is the benefit for me to learn that my friend is looking for a surfing instructor in Alacati[15], in the middle of my work. Isn't this vulgarity?"

Frankly speaking, we can divide people who are asking this type of questions into two groups. First group: People who know how to use this process for their own benefit and who have learned and internalized social media. Second group: People who did not understand social media and who do not know how to deal with it since they don't know how to use it.

People who use social media intensely do not care much about this kind of updates in the statuses of their friends. But of course there is also a crazy crowd who turns every status update, shared photos or written comments into an obsession.

Individuals are able to set their own message display preferences in social media. They can decide whose statuses are going to be seen in their timeline and whose not. In short, these processes are customizable. It is already possible to do that in all the mobile phones. You can enable your smart phone to inform you the @ mentions of you in Twitter by message. Or vice versa... You can read these messages whenever you want without being distracted while doing something else.

The key to social media is the state of being in communication with the people you want to have a relation in an easy and natural way. Now someone might say "I don't have enough time during the day, how can I follow people or how can I inform these people about myself during the day continuously? I cannot waste my time like this!"

Let me give you the special secret of this book: Killing time in Facebook and social media actually renders you more efficient.

I feel sorry for the organizations which block or prohibit social media access of their employees in the name of efficiency. If you have ever understood how much time your employees lost without social media, you would have made it compulsory for them to spend at least two hours in Facebook on a daily basis to make them more efficient.

FOR THE ONES RESISTING TO CHANGE

My son is five years old. He has been using my iPhone since he was one and a half years old. Isn't it interesting? Of course he doesn't know how to read and write and is not able to make searches. But he is able to change the screen with a funny hand gesture in order to reach the application he wants. He knows perfectly well to open the application he wants (these are mostly games of course), to choose a level and play, and then to close these. Every night he says "Daddy, could you give me your A'fon" and plays the games he likes. When he gets bored with the games he asks "Daddy, can you download me new games?" He also knows that the games are downloaded from Internet. Even I am surprised that he understands what the Internet is. When my child grows up, he would not be able to conceive a world without

Internet. Just as we are not able to conceive a world without automobile.

OK, let's not go that far in the past. It has not been such a long time for this one I will ask: Are you able to conceive of a business life without e-mails?

I was in senior high school when I met Internet. Now, I feel terrified when I see little girls who are text messaging without even looking to their fingers writing the text in the speed of light, as it were. According to a survey, teenage girls who are between 14-17 years old are far more ahead than the boys in the same age group with the average of one hundred text messages daily vs. thirty text messages. As of May 2010, 72% of the adults are sending/receiving ten text messages daily. I am sure that these figures will increase. Today, even my father has a Facebook account and he also follows everybody's status updates in the family. He comments to our posts and posts his own shares.

Today, we can only compare the influence of social media starting with Web 2.0 technology on marketing communications with the influence of printing technology on business life years ago. You will find information related to the right usage of social media in the following chapters of the book but first I have a few words for the ones who are still resisting to the change and who do not want to give up their habits.

EXCUSES ARE ENDLESS FOR THE ONES LOOKING FOR THEM

There are many excuses for the people who are still shying away from social media according to researches as well as based on my own experiences. I have sorted out these excuses and commented about them.

"THE MEASUREMENTS ON SOCIAL MEDIA ARE NOT RELIABLE."

Yes, how nice. Let's suppose that there are forty million TVs in Turkey for the population of seventy million. So, you think that making generalizations based on the rating devices installed in 5 thousand houses in total is reliable, huh? Honestly, I don't think they are reliable at all. This kind of measurement means that 99% of the country is not taken into account. I studied business management and I respect to those who take a sample at this rate and make measurements accordingly. But my other identity, the marketing professional, would continue to wonder about what the remaining 99% is doing. Moreover, I have never encountered a house with a rating device in my whole life. I don't find it satisfying to think that these people wait for the programs with the remote control in their hands.

Similarly, you would think that it is really measurable to give one-page ads worth between 5,000-20,000 TL to a monthly magazine which supposedly has a circulation of 100 thousand even when you cannot even be sure that your ad is going to be seen, wouldn't you?

I can guarantee that you would have a much more precise and measurable result in social media with the one fifth of the budget you would spend in conventional media.

People exist with their real identities on Facebook. 95% of Internet users in Turkey have Facebook accounts. So, if I am going to run a diaper campaign on Facebook, I am able to choose only women as my target group and show my ads to them. In addition, I can select the marital status of these women as married. Moreover, I can choose to show my ads only to women who are twenty five years and older. If I want, I can specify the education levels of these women as college graduates. Also, I can make my ads to appear in the pages of specific communities of women. I can narrow the field down further based on demographical information. Do I need to say more?

If this is not enough, I can mention that I can follow how many times an ad was displayed, how many clicks it got after all these display times as daily reports or simultaneously.

I ask you again; so do you still think that TVs and conventional media are more reliable than Internet?

"IT IS NOT CLEAR HOW THE INVESTMENT WILL RETURN."

70% of the people consult their family and friends while making their purchasing decision. Well, how are these people communicating with family and friends in the last two or three years? Of course on social networks such as Facebook, Twitter etc. when people face an option, they make their purchasing decision as long as they can relate it to somebody they know. Facebook reports that 60% of Internet users enter social networks and half of them are engaging in this act every day.

There is a reality marketing professionals know too well; money is where the community is. Nowadays people are in social media fast and noisily. They talk to each other, share their likes, tell their stories, and write about their experiences. Social media has more influence in forming the interactions which can create associations related to purchasing when compared to conventional media. Additionally, in this medium, the communication always works in two ways. You say something with your brand, you get an answer. You ask a question, you get an answer. You give an answer, you get a question.

Social media enables people to see brand preferences of their family and friends and their interactions with the brand. And it offers more opportunity in the name of forming personal associations that could lead to purchasing decisions in doing so.

"WE NEED TO HAVE CONTROL OVER THE THINGS THAT ARE BEING TOLD ABOUT US."

Many companies I've interviewed still resist opening a Facebook page, writing on blogs, opening a Twitter account, in short being present in social media. The only reason for that, of course, is the thought of in case a customer sends negative comments or competition sabotages their pages constantly with bad comments.

"If we would have a Facebook account, talks we don't want would be going on about us and since this message is on the crazy nutty social media which we don't have any control over, we cannot obviate this."

Yes, this is exactly how the understanding is.

Yet, you already don't have control over your message anymore company owners! That ship has already sailed. Now, you want it or not, many people are talking, writing about and criticizing your product or service on social media.

Why are you afraid of opening a page on Facebook? What would happen if your customers post negative comments on your page? If you don't open your page, they can open pages in your name and talk about you negatively or positively as they want. In fact, they are already talking now.

You have to make a choice here. Would you prefer your customers to send their messages to a place in such a way that you won't even have the opportunity to answer? Or would you prefer them sending messages to a place in which you can be included in the dialogue, answer your customer's complaint, have the opportunity to transform a negative attitude to a positive one?

Knowing the complaints of your unhappy customers would give you the advantage to be able to satisfy their needs. The reason for the customer to contact you about a negative outcome of the interaction between you two is that they still are hopeful about you. Think of an angry customer who is so offended that they do not even say anything or contact you. The real fear should be the customers who had a bad experience and went away to never come back again without saying a word.

Social media provides a beautiful opportunity to prevent this from happening.

"I THINK IT IS A PASSING FANCY."

So continue to think that way. Social media is a massive socio-economical change. Although dynamics of marketing applied for centuries are still valid, social media has transformed the ways of business and the expectations of people completely. TV campaigns worth millions of liras are no longer the key factor to trigger purchasing behavior. The new king is the access to products and services using social media tools.

In 1922, radio began to be a new platform for the companies to conduct ad campaigns. Then companies waited more than twenty years, until 1950s for TV to offer them a new opportunity. Another forty years needed to pass for Internet to come. Thirty eight years passed until radio reached 150 million people, TV spent thirteen years to reach the same numbers; Internet, on the other hand, reached 150 million people in only five years. I would like to draw your attention on how increasingly fast they all get accepted. Web 2.0 is an Internet revolution. I suppose it would be needles for me to ask how long it took for Facebook or Twitter to universalize. The game becomes faster every passing day.

Merriam-Webster, the most prestigious dictionary of the world, has already included Twitter and "Tweet" as words in its dictionary.

Social media has changed the game in a very short time by transforming the rules of today with the ways of communication that we wouldn't be able to imagine ten years ago.

Let's suppose that we are going to launch a new product. You cannot do this without social media today. Here I can only acknowledge this fact; wagons could change in time when they are replaced by better ones (Facebook, Twitter, YouTube) but the train we ride is always the same: what changes is the train of the mode of communication.

"I DON'T HAVE ENOUGH TIME TO FOLLOW OR MONEY TO PAY TO ANOTHER TO HANDLE THIS."

If you have a one-person company or you are a small business, you won't have much chance in terms of costs or currency anyway. You have to follow the talks going around you and get involved in the dialogue. Of course if you don't care, that's quite another story.

Now the time of sparing your interest for your best and the most profitable customer with the best turnover rate is over. Both the best money spenders and the random encounters are in the same ecosystem. All of them live in an ecosystem in which your attitudes could be annunciated to your existing and potential customers rapidly. You have to create a way of talking about your brand in social media and lay a foundation. When you start to get good results with this foundation in time, you will eventually need an assistant.

Once upon a time, companies were finding it sufficient to employ only one person in their IT (Information Technologies) departments. This job's importance was understood in time and the number of people working in IT departments also started to increase.

The same thing applies to social media today; you will start to increase the number of the people you employ in your social media department as you start to understand that this job is actually a job which requires quite a lot of work and has a high rate of return on investment.

In addition, this department won't be conducting some regular marketing operation. Your organization's "Customer Relationship Management – CRM" infrastructure should also be linked to this department. Therefore "Social Media" department may even become the largest department or the field with the highest number of employee in your organization. It is enough for you to know how to delegate and to create the required environment for everybody enabling them to show their own colors. Otherwise, you may hit a wall many times until you understand social media processes in a right way.

"WE ARE BETTER WITHOUT IT; BESIDES WE HAVE TRIED BUT IT DOESN'T WORK."

If you can say this, this means you've already lost your competitive identity as a company. In this case I would recommend you to review the business you are conducting all over again. A company which is satisfied with itself so as to think that everything is "good" is a company which deserves to go down.

How can you say about something you haven't tried that it is not a "good" thing? Moreover, there is nothing to say to the ones declaring that they have tried but it didn't work. This is probably due to the executives who spent 2-3 months for this job and concluded with an early judgment when they didn't see any increase in numbers or wasn't able to increase their web traffic adequately. "It doesn't work."

Of course there is no need to accuse managers at this point; managers are always rewarded based on their short-term operations. The preference in this case is to collect ripe apples on the tree. Who would plant new apple trees, labor for their growth and wait for the different kinds of apples to grow, right? On the other hand, if the managers were to be rewarded for long-term project development, they would be able to get out of their plane and understand social media's importance within the whole picture.

The truth is social media processes are definitely not short distance races. On the contrary, they are marathons. They are long-term projects. They must be planned for a long period of time and penetrate into all the units of an organization. The ones who deploy themselves in their positions while digging their trenches and start working by participating in dialogues and creating content will come out ahead in this business. Patience must not be forgotten as well. This business requires resoluteness. Of course the ones who act rapidly and who understand the long-termed nature of the work to be done will achieve significant benefits in time.

This truth was understood even by my relatively small scale customers who have 3 to 10 employees and they started to get results at the end of one year. Believe me; if you try and cannot get any results, you have not understood exactly what social media is for.

"IT IS NOTHING BUT A PLATFORM THAT ENABLES MY COMPETITORS TO ABUSE ME MORE EASILY."

Yes, your competitors as well could go to your Facebook page and write negative comments. But be sure that, they will understand within the shortest time that it is to their benefit to get their own social media businesses in order rather than fiddling with you while your followers there are increasing in number in an affirmative way. Besides this risk always exists for all communication channels you have in your disposal.

Sure, Facebook or Twitter pages of yours won't only be liked by your competitors. Fans of your brand and your customers who would talk in your name would also start to increase in number in the same community. Your competitors' childish moves would be eliminated by your representatives as the number of your representatives increases and your communication with them strengthens.

Oh and one more thing; cowards die many times before their deaths!

"SOCIAL MEDIA IS ONLY USEFUL FOR TECHNOLOGY COMPANIES."

I also am aware that an armature company and a logistics company have totally different business models and processes. But I also know that the job of an armature company is not to sell armature to everyone and every house but only to the ones who have armature needs. This applies for a logistics company as well. It doesn't matter whether you offer products/services that reach to the final consumer or use mediators in between. Your strongest marketing feature is to be able to access people who might have these potential needs. Social media comes to play at this very point.

Armature is not your essential key word when selling armatures. Hotels and buildings, modifications, parks, construction and architecture are the real key words that you must converse around.

The ones who think that social media is only useful for newly established companies or technology companies are mistaken. A survey shows that 40% of the fastest growing technology firms and the ones which have Twitter accounts never replied to the messages they have been sent. What a shame!

If you are passionate about your product or service, you will be more in sight for your existing customers by talking in social media and will also attract potential customers to yourself like a magnet.

You will become an opinion leader through the speeches you give in your field of expertise and the answers you come up with for the ones asking questions and in time, you will be regarded as a person of distinction as being a real expert in the field. Of course you will be the one preferred after all these works.

In the future, the companies which have a real "relationship capital" in social media will be successful. Social media provides a wonderful opportunity without the need to have an ability to form a relationship intellectually.

People will be looking for good manners, honest, sincere and personal things. They will prefer to engage in conversations with humans rather than computers or interactive voice response. Moreover they will prefer doing this through the easiest method: social media.

HOW DOES INFORMATION DISSEMINATE?

How does news spread? I want to give a recent experience of mine as an example. I mentioned before that newspapers and magazines lose blood every passing year. The smart journalists are already positioning themselves in social media. Some of them are also creating content online while distributing these via Twitter just as they happen.

When Ministry of Foreign Affairs was declaring Turkey's policy about Israel right after the Blue Marmara event, DipNot, which is a competitive news portal in social media, was already entering the news into its website and announcing this via related social networks. Immediately I saw that a friend of mine retweeted DipNot's tweet to his 300 friend. Just one minute later, I saw Radikal's columnist Ezgi Basaran's tweet which summarized the whole series of events and I retweeted her tweet to my 550 followers. The conversation got heated. 3 minutes later New York Times tweeted about the matter. People were sharing this news in blogs and micro blogs. Hundreds of people interested in diplomacy started to write their opinions about the matter with critiques and the strategies to come. Within 1 hour after the actual event, the matter had thousands of times more content on Internet than TV channels and printed media were able to produce. 1 hour later, we learned that the announcement made by the Ministry of Foreign Affairs before United Nations' Report arrived was due the report's leaking into New York Times. Do I need to say where this leakage resulted from? I assume everybody has heard about Wikileaks.[16] Well, this was a similar leakage. And all these developments took place in just 2 hours.

As you see, everything develops in a dizzying speed. Guess where does the journalist working on the matter refers first to get information in order to write the news on the next day's paper.

You guessed it right: Google.

So what does this journalist do in Google? Of course, just the same things I did. He looks to the articles written about this matter before; he follows what everybody talked and what everybody still talking about; then starts to compile these.

On the other hand, tens of ordinary blog writers write about the matter as they like just because they are interested in it.

A blog writer probably does the following as of the moment he completes the article (I call this thinking as a real time publisher):

1. From his subscriptions like Twitter, RSS (real simple indication) feeds and with the help of filtration software that filtrates the related tags (words), he finds the related articles and reads them.
2. Starts writing, completes the article and edits it.
3. When he is sure and publishes it, he shares it with his 300 friends on Facebook, also with his 100 followers on Twitter.
4. His forty friends/followers read it.
5. His twenty friends/followers share it again on their own profiles/accounts.
6. His ten friends/followers rate and tag the article on social media "bookmark" websites. (e.g.; Delicious, DIGG, Reddit).
7. Some websites and blogs give links to the article or republish it on their own blogs.
8. Similar steps from step one to step six continue to be repeated over and over.

Search engines read these social bookmarks and links and give high ratings to these within the news found in the organic search results. A blog article tagged with the words "Sanction to Israel" is able to draw more interest than the news written by any other online newspaper.

In short, high quality content and correct social media construct could even get you ahead of online newspapers. In this case, you can witness that even conventional media itself follows you.

This situation led newspapers and magazines to review their business models all over again. In 2008 American PC Magazine announced that it will not be printed again. Magazine carried all its operations to Internet and PC Magazine called itself PC Mag in the online world. This change was necessary since advertisement revenues were in a decrease although it was still good at that time. Moreover PC Mag made this decision in a period when it wasn't losing money.

Conventional newspapers and magazines should know by now that people expect to be informed about news by their friends or the websites there are members of.

THE POWER OF A BLOG POST

I had an experience in 2009 to prove me that I am actually right. A magazine, which loves to make lists of everything in fifties or hundreds, published an article on 50 most expensive painters in Turkey. As a person who was making extensive researches on art market in those days and as I believed that I have a word or two to say on plastic arts in Turkey, I wrote a critique about that list and I published this article on Artimetre.com, an amateur art blog of which I was the editor back then. After publishing this article, I immediately started to share it on social networks. I had 70 or so Twitter followers at those days. And Artimetre.com had a group of 150 on Facebook.

2 hours later I published the article, they called me from this world famous magazine. The woman on the other end of the phone said "Our chief editor wants to speak with you." No sooner had I said "OK" than I was talking with the chief editor of the magazine. I remember our conversation being as heated as it was mutually polite. In short, chief editor told me that my article was a little too much cruel and tried to explain that the method they used for sorting out the list was very valid. My opinion about the article didn't change a bit no matter what she said, but she had a point, I give her that. My critique's title was really cruel but not least dangerous. (I won't write it here) So that when you Googled the chief editor's name just 6 hours later I had written it, my article was coming second from the top. Chief Editor said that if I don't change this title, her journalism career would be at stake. In other words, I would be quarreling with her bread and butter.

She was right. I had a very powerful weapon in my hand. I knew how influential Google was already but I was now realizing how fast social media could be and how it is being digested immediately. I was not a journalist. If there was a journalism ethics, I apparently had violated that. Additionally, I never wanted to strand her.

Still, there was something I liked in this situation; when one presented high quality and original content on the Internet, one's content was always finding its target. And with a point shot.

I asked to the chief editor: "How and from whom you've heard about this critique in such a short time?"

The answer: "My friends have read it on Twitter, they told me." I immediately started to construct the social media infrastructures of the brands, the sales and marketing operations of which I was conducting. I tested my first plans on Harbiyiyorum.com in which I was free enough to do it my way.

SEARCH ENGINES AND SOCIAL MEDIA

Fast and cheap information sharing is the strongest suit of Internet but it is also its biggest weakness. Search engines will continue to find the truest results for people's needs within trillions of data byte today and in the future. The biggest obstacle at this point is people's inability to define correctly what they are looking for. For example, if you write "Mother's Day Gift for My One and Only Mother" on a search engine, you would find some useful titles for sure but the results would be confusing most of the time. Moreover, if the content you are looking for doesn't appear in the first page of the search results, you would probably also be in the majority of 95% who doesn't view the second page.

Making your searches more specific could help if you

want your searches to have more useful results. Save that, in order to reach specific information within so many results, you will need a magic wand. I call this wand "Social Media."

Search engines bring us the results we desire by understanding our personal needs more clearly with each passing day. High tech search engines are able to understand that the target is the celebrity "Paris Hilton" when a teenager searches for "Paris Hilton" and a room at Hilton Hotel in Paris is what matters when my mother-in-law searches for "Paris Hilton".

These are nice developments but when one searches for generic titles such as "soap" or "car", the results would be the same as everyone's results. While this type of semantic improvements go on in search engines - and I can say that it doesn't go very fast due to the monopoly in the market; Google just enjoys this power -, you could actually reach the real result for your search if you make a specific search such as "The Best Roast Chicken in Istanbul."

This book is mainly about social media but search engines and social media are so much interrelated in digital marketing communications that they cannot be thought separately. And here is another truth; while search engines are algorithmic and mathematical structures, social media instruments behave in a way much closer to the emotional center of the individual.

In other words, we can say that search engines are the logic and social media is the spirit of the whole thing.

If people are looking for the academic or gathering data for a serious research, they would look in Wikipedia on the Internet world which becomes more niche everyday. Or if they are looking for some fun, searching for celebrities or singers, they would go into Facebook or MySpace. StumbleUpon, Delicious, Digg and such social bookmarking sites would be the direction to find out the most popular titles about a subject.

That is why Google does not see other search engines (Yahoo, MSN, Yandex etc.) as its rivals. The strongest rival of Google is social media itself. This was the reason behind Google's YouTube acquisition. This is why it continually launches new products under the title of "our social networks".

SOCIAL SEARCH WARS

Google and other search engines are perfectly aware of this change and they especially care about the increasing social aspect of every new product they introduce. If we make a short visit to the recent past we can see many social media move Google made;

Google Search Wiki at the beginning of 2009 (an algorithm in which page ranks of search results are determined by people) the comment feature for search results, e-mail, message, chat, wikis etc., Google Wave to improve the integration, followed by Google +1 and now Google Plus. (i.e. Google Facebook)

Old and new players are challenging each other on the arena to win the social search wars.

Even though I see that Google has introduced effective tools such as Google Plus, I don't believe that a product which was launched and marketed with "There is no place, I am making room for very special friends" logic could dethrone Facebook.

Google is a brand constructed on logic, algorithms and mathematic genius from the very beginning. Facebook, on the other hand, takes shape around emotional center from the beginning.

The two archetypes send quite different signals to our subconscious. One is Santa Claus who surprises and entertains us; other is Pythagoras who continuously presents us mathematical theories.

We must separate the wheat from the chaff.

Yes, after all this situation assessment and sermon about the changes social media created in our lives now is the time for the route assessment... What kind of a route we must take in social media? Where should we be? Which media are for your brand? How can you highlight your brand in social media? How can you get more likes on Facebook? Who is social media expert? What is the true nature of social media? How can Twitter be used effectively in marketing communications?

I've been doing research for almost 2 years to find out the answers of such questions. I will draw you a road map on how to use social media in marketing communications in the following chapter of the book. Just as I did for the firms I consult, people I train and Harbiyiyorum.com.

And here we go...

CHAPTER 2

Content, Sincerity And The First Step

IF YOU HAVE A PRODUCT OR A SERVICE TO OFFER, that means you also have content to be constituted in social media. But you need to be really passionate about the thing of which you are creating. I call your attention: You need to be passionate, not an expert. This passion of yours would make you an expert in time anyway. Any discourse on a shaky ground and without support will be easily noticed by your audience on social media. This requires you to be honest on every subject you create the content of.

If you are a real estate agent, you would have hundreds of things to say about your region or real estates in your region. If you are interested in art, you would certainly have things to say on art market.

If you have things to say on your product or service, you have to do this with sincerity. By the way, it is important that your product or service is something really useful as well. Let's suppose that you just launched an energy drink - those usually taste like syrup - and if it tastes really bad, your sincerity would already be negated. Or if you are building your content on inadequately prepared information, you wouldn't have much chance on social media.

In such a case, it is hard for you to have a chance even in the normal world let alone social media.

Do not try to show your product or service different than it is. You would be getting a very fast response in such a case on social media and the reaction you get could ruin all your plans.

So, since you are sure of your product/service/hobby and your passion, you now have to make as much research as you can and transform your content to a sincere expression blended with information. And where would you be publishing this content?

Of course on a blog you will start...

BLOGS

I call them "network diaries". According to Wikipedia, these are diary like websites which are prepared by people without the requirement of technical knowledge who write about the things they want the way they want.

I would like to develop this description a little further. Since the extent of it has gone beyond the diary. Firstly, we always think of "writing" when we think of diaries. Whereas there are three formats you can publish on your Internet blog. These are image, audio and text. Whatever production you produce for the content, you can use each of them in different formats or combine them to support each other.

In other words, you can add a few lines under the video you publish on your blog for example. Secondly, blogs are replacing classical websites increasingly every passing day.

This is my theory but here is the truth; blogs are extensively interactive websites which are easy to use, more update able, and compatible with social media and you can open and start to enter content in it in 3 minutes without the need of a graphical designer/programmer.

You cannot do this with your normal websites (of course provided that your website doesn't have a blog infrastructure.) Today, even the popular websites use blog infrastructure when they are marketed to the companies with content management. Your eyes would be popping out of your head probably if somebody said that they are building blog infrastructure for the website your corporation is paying to have made. The truth is most of the time it works like this nowadays.

THE PERIOD OF ELABORATE WEBSITES IS OVER

If you don't have an e-trade website, the websites with two pages of mission and vision parts, one-sided description of product and service, which has a message form that doesn't assure you about the delivery of your message without a working contact section are unfortunately extinguishing.

How many of us today bother to read the mission and vision information of a firm by entering to their corporate website? I, personally, go to a corporate website only to get the phone or address information, if any. I am not at all interested in the rest of the pages. Pages which are boring and full of unnecessary information. Without communication, deserted and orphan...

Also if I want to get information about a firm other than the contact information, I would Google it. I would look for what is being said on social media or in the blogs about the company. That is why I recommend to the corporations I consult that they should only make a single page with their address and phone information if they are going to renew their websites. And I say that changing background pictures now and again would be enough for update as we are already publishing the content on social media. And everything would be good to go once they give a nice link to social media platforms I will be discussing later from their website.

There are two examples exactly like this which have directed to their social networks from their own websites:

the confectioner Skittles from abroad and Cast Office from Turkey. Both of them have all their communications directed to their social accounts. Cast Office has comfortably written "You can follow your business or contact us for your applications on our Facebook page" on its webpage with an arrow. What a comfort and what a joy!

Ye firms! Let the people who want to get informed more about you reach you via their social networks. Adapt yourself to a period in which everything gets easier everyday and the fields of expertise create their own ecosystems according to their branches.

Especially, I am at a loss for words for the fancy websites which do not like search engines (it is better not to search for it in search engines), with too much going on and which are ultra live and incredibly cool. It is not so much possible for the flash websites to be found on search engines and it is even more impossible on smart phones. Advertisement agencies may recommend you very cool, ultra supersonic websites with videos on the background etc. Do not give such websites much credit if you want your product or service to be found on search engines. But if you say that you have such a dream, that you must have such a website, I have nothing much to say to you.

In future, flash websites will exist for very artistic purposes, just for prestige and if the owners do not care for it to be found on Google. Flash is already loosing its validity and is being replaced with HTML5 tech. You should go on with HTML websites if you care about your content being found and try to gain money from the sales of your service like me.

Let's proceed with creating a blog after retiring your websites and announcing them as "Honorary Presidents" of your Executive Board. There are many options for us but I will explain the main way to take.

The thing for you to do is very simple if you want to

open a blog in five minutes and don't want to spend any money on this (just as I did with Harbiyiyorum in the beginning):
- www.blogger.com
- www.wordpress.com
- www.tumblr.com

Enter one of the above websites. This list contains the most popular and preferred free blog services with tens of thousands of writers. I had experiences with each one of them. In addition, all of these websites support different languages. Now, I continue with all these services except Blogger - and I will explain why I stopped using Blogger in a minute.

If the name for your product or service is already defined, you can have such a web address in 2 minutes and free of charge.

Let's say that we defined the name of our products as Harbiyiyorum. In this case, below are the website addresses you can get depending on the blog service provider: (Below adresses do not exist!)
- www.harbiyiyorum.blogspot.com
- www.harbiyiyorum.wordpress.com
- www.harbiyiyorum.tumblr.com

I would like to mention here that, all these service providers give you the website name as seen above free of charge and the hosting service, the hosting of the content you produce, is also given free of charge.

WHICH BLOG?

Now, if you ask me which one is my favorite as a person who already have used all of these services, as of now (08.05.2012) I would say that it is Tumblr.[17] Tumblr keeps impressing me with its ready designs, the simple interface for content entries, the ease of sharing, the feature that allows you to use the content you liked from other Tumblr blogs (re-blog), the incredible compatibility with smart phones and its software developed for smart phones, the integration with other social networks etc. and much more. Tumblr have come a long way in being a real phenomenon within the blog world despite its late establishment in 2007.

Even though I have begun Harbiyiyorum and my other blogs on Blogger initially, it was the prohibition of access that made me stop using Blogger.com. A prohibition came in 2009 for the first time. Then another came in 2011. There was a prohibition of access for all the websites with .blogspot extensions due to a sports broadcast. I compare it to this: There is only one pest in a field and to get rid of it, you put the whole field on fire! People were seeing "Access to this website is prohibited with the court decision" with large fonts when they tried to enter to Harbiyiyorum. How would they know? For I thought I was under suspicion as if I committed a crime and wrote pornographic food articles, I immediately started to search for other blog services to avoid this situation. And I made radical changes as a result of my research.

Actually, the only reason for me to start a blog on Blogger which was initially established by Pyra Labs, was its being acquired by Google in 2003. Whatever my content would be, I was sure that Google would prioritize a blog hosted by Blogger. In time I arrived to the conclusion that Google cannot have such a policy. For the job of Google was to give people the most accurate information in relation with what they are looking for. Constituting a foundation for such a duality for a firm based on such a principle would damage its credibility; moreover it wouldn't be ethical at all. (Still I cannot get rid of this doubt of mine; who would a person be of more help to: one's own child or other's children?)

At the end, due to the censorship, I needed to immediately remove Harbiyiyorum from the ecosystem with Blogspot extension and this would have to be solved in a professional manner.

Wordpress could be established with the domain redirection you get on the host which would be hosting your content. As a matter of fact, Wordpress is the leader for this kind of blogs. So I have redirected the domain name of www.harbiyiyorum.com to a server I rented and moved my blog to an ecosystem in which the baby won't be thrown out with the bathwater. Now, people entering to Harbiyiyorum.com will see a website which has its own domain name without any extension anywhere. This website is actually a blog with "Wordpress Blog" infrastructure. If you remember what I've said before, I meant exactly this when I mentioned the websites are being created with the blog infrastructure. My website is a blog but it doesn't have an extension of .wordpress or .blogspot. Its only difference from the other blogs is that now I have a professional blog. If professionalism is mentioned somewhere, it means taking or giving money. Now I hold the position of the payer. In other words I pay a yearly fee for hosting to my service provider. The yearly price is around 50-100 USD together with the domain name. I am really a professional. (Really?!)

The only difference between any regular blog and a professional blog is that you pay for one of them.

I have moved my personal blog (www.salihseckinsevinc.com) in the same way from Blogger to Tumblr this time. I thought Tumblr as a concept was more compatible with my personal brand and more functional. My personal blog is still not professional but since I already have my own domain name, I am able to redirect to my address, **http://salihseckinsevinc.tumblr.com**. Yet, I don't pay anything for content hosting/server as it is for Harbiyiyorum.com. But again, I'll be moving to Wordpress soon. (I moved already! 01.11.2013)

Whether you pay for your blog or not, the only thing to make you appear on the top in the search engines will be the content you produce. Search engines do not look if you're paying for your blogs or not, they only look to your content.

CREATING CONTENT FOR YOUR BLOG

What does Google do technically? How much time does it take for the robots to visit my site? How would Google love my website more? This are the details I wouldn't understand as an expert of SEO (Search Engine Optimization) but the first question I ask myself as a marketing communications expert would be "How would I search for information I need as an individual on Google?" And, thinking from the perspective of the content producer, I would act on the question of "How would I produce high quality and different content?"

The first thing to do when you produce content for your blog is to choose the format you will be publishing in. There are three options: text, audio and image & video. Of course the determining factor here would be the form of the content you will be producing. In some cases these three could be combined but general practice is to move on a standard format at a certain rate. Techcrunch[18] or Sosyalmedyanedir[19] could be given as examples of the blogs with text format. On the other hand, Bikafalar[20] could give an idea about the examples of video blogs.

No matter which format you use, your priority should be to create quality content for your blog to be successful. You have to maintain the continuous production of content (if you neglect it, it will fade away and die like a flower which was not given water) and you have to have the qualifications to be able to produce content continuously in the subjects that you know and feel passionate about.

The successful bloggers' common feature is the continuous writing. Whether you write one or five article in a month, it doesn't matter. It is enough to maintain this writing period as it is.

Of course you would have to be well prepared about whatever it is you are talking about or the content you produce. No matter how well you talk about it, if what you are talking about is trash, the content you produce will take its place as trash in the Internet universe as well.

You can make your process of learning a part of your content too. At the end, you would be acting according to social media spirit as much as you are sincere. You don not need to express everything perfectly. If you are a perfectionist "I'm ready" point may never come.

There are blogs in which people tell "how they cannot cook" on the contrary of professional recipe websites abroad. An example to this is Amy Chow's blog. It is truly a great site. Amy's video blog "Stupidly Simple Snacks" has already become a phenomenon on Internet.

It is safe to produce content similar to what is generally done but it is ordinary and it doesn't draw attention. Always pursue the different.

The more original your content is, the more clicks your blog posts will receive. The originality of the product you are writing about will trigger more clicks. For example, if you have a sandwich shop and name the most expensive sandwich of your "Gym Shoe" as Sun Submarine in Chicago has done, the content you will produce about this sandwich on your blog will surely break a hit record.

Today if you want to find a mobile app development firm, you will probably write "Mobile App Development Firms" on Google and search. If you are to write an article titled "7 Firms Developing Mobile Apps in Turkey" as I did, you will probably reach hundreds of potential customers who made a Google search like this.

Do I need to say that I have received phones from many potential customers saying "We want to develop mobile apps" after I wrote that article?

What's important is to see the content as a need from the perspective of consumer and produce the content as fast as possible. Result: Original content always works.

CORPORATE BLOGS

Unfortunately, many firms I see the examples of start blogs just because there is a blog trend.

First and foremost, the corporations have to get rid of the assumption that they won't be receiving feedback just as it is with the conventional advertisement media where they are not encountering their customers face to face.

We are talking about an interactive medium when we say blog. You have to help people to get into an interaction with you. Forget about the ads you have been giving to newspapers and TVs and about this kind of marketing approach. Here, there is a new, evolved communication model. Be as creative as you want in a classical medium, juggle six things at the same time, at the end you are saying "My product is great and buy this!" If you are going to constantly talk about your products or services on your blog, I have to say you are on the wrong path from the beginning (of course if you don't have extreme products such as Gym Shoe.) Sorry, but it won't work to constantly polish your goods here.

WHERE ARE THOSE OLD FRIENDS?

Everybody has probably had friends who constantly talk about themselves. You too surely had one. You HAD once, right? Really, where are those friends now? How long can you listen to someone who is constantly talking about themselves or how long you can sustain such a friendship?

I, personally, wasn't able to put up with any one of them! Even though I tried to bear them, natural selection wouldn't let me.

We can call a relationship healthy as long as it is reciprocal. Of course you are going to talk about yourself when you are with your friends and tell them what you've been up to. Yet, you have to take a breath at the end and ask "So how have you been? What you've been up to?" Now, that is real friendship.

And things work exactly like this in social media.

Therefore, a blog on which comments are blocked is not really a blog. More precisely, it is nothing more than a conventional advertisement medium on which a healthy communication could never happen.

In any case, brands have to permit comments being written under their posts and every brand should try to have different elements outside of their own brand news.

Blogs are the main bases for all kinds of advertisement and promotion campaigns of a brand. You cannot tumble things over whenever you want on your website about your marketing operations but you can start an online campaign in three minutes on your blog and share this on different social networks in the next ten minutes.

So how does corporate blog differ than personal blog? Of course you can add aesthetic elements characteristic to your corporation in terms of visual design. Still, I recommend you instruct your graphic designers not to draw too much away from a blog atmosphere when they are working on a special design for your corporation. The best format is always the known one; the one in which the articles are listed from the top to the bottom with archives and categories. By the way, there is no need to indicate "blog" in the beginning or the end of your domain name. Blog is the name of a specific format and you can use any domain name you like for your blog. Actually, Citroen's blog is a good example for this. They have a separate domain name for their blog pages.

Below are examples of blogs of various corporations serving in different industries:
http://blog.markafoni.com/
http://dahabaska.com/blog/
http://www.trcitroen.com/
http://blog.microsoft.com.tr/

Now, hang on to your hat! I am announcing what is indispensable for your corporate blog: A writer or a group of writers who are able to write continuously and produce high quality content. You can delegate someone from inside, you can write yourself or you can get support from agencies and copywriters. All three options require acting with the understanding of marketing and publishing and producing content according to this.

JUST START

During the conferences I participate, I encounter many people who are willing to write on blogs but do not know where to start. They come to me with the following questions in general:
- I cannot decide what to write.
- I am interested in food and marketing; can I publish both on the same blog?
- There are many things I want to write about, I cannot decide where to start!

I usually answer as follows: It is enough for you to just start writing about your field of interest. Later, as the number of your posts increases, you can start different blogs, you can say "writing is not my thing, video expresses my thoughts better" or you can decide that it is not your thing at all; it all depends on you!

Actually, producing original content for the blog is also something that will develop in time as you write on your blog. You are not writing for a magazine at the end. Your post will not stay there, printed forever. You have the opportunity to edit your posts as much as you like. I can honestly confess; I edit my blog posts tens of times until they are in their final shape. Even when I say "That is it!"

I experience nice things. My readers warn me about the places I should edit on the post. And this is the best part of the communication on social media.

Let people critique you, correct your errors, contribute to your posts, and write their own comments. Your purpose at the end is to create interactivity. You want people to read your posts and visit your blog more often, don't you?

Blogs are the main bases for you to create your content (campaign, product launch, promotion, announcement etc.). Everything that you are going to share on social media would be content without an address if there were no blogs. I can say for any brand and corporation that a social media strategy without a blog on the center is doomed to fail.

As a corporation, we announce a product launch first and foremost on our own blog. Later, we share this content proportionately on social networks. Our blog is always in the center of our all marketing communications strategy whether it is conventional or printed. This way, we ensure continuous interactivity with our audience and put ourselves forth as the first source of reference on the matter in search engines.

Yes, since now you have a blog and made it your main base, we can continue towards other social media networks starting from this main base.

Don't forget, now everybody is a publisher and the age is the age of blogs.

FACEBOOK

When Facebook was established by students from Harvard in 2004, I was operating in a quite different field away from Internet. I became familiar with Facebook in 2007. Myspace[21] drew my attention more before that. It was quite normal for Myspace to draw my attention since Myspace was more like a fun social network for music bands to come together and I was into music. Myspace still maintains this character.

When Facebook started to slowly appear in Turkey in 2007, the first impression was that it enabled people to easily find their old friends with whom they have lost contact and facilitated communication with them. Additionally, as our number of friends here increased, everybody was able to see what everybody was doing and communicate with each other.

As the population on Facebook increased and as people started to understand more of the benefits of communication on Facebook, the motivation for the brands to use this for their benefit started to arise. The first practice for brands, even though it was wrong, was to open accounts just as personal profiles and send friendship requests to people. This was naturally against Facebook's logic. So Facebook started "Groups" for corporate bodies for the first time. It was possible to gather people with the same interest together in groups and share posts with all the group members as well as send messages to all of them.

When this message sending started to turn into SPAM in time, Facebook put some limitations on groups and announced "Pages" this time. Pages consisted of the people who "Like" the brands and corporations; they were working with a different algorithm and had a similar structure to personal accounts while being functional and manageable. Corporate bodies flowed in the "Pages" immediately upon Facebook's announcement. For they knew the money was where people were. Therefore, there was an urgent need of integrating this new communication medium into their marketing activities. This happened incredibly fast of course. Brands started to increase their 'likes' on their Facebook pages as they were integrating their classical marketing operations here.

Of course, agencies which were at the stage of digitalization had to take action about social media and they also stepped up quickly.

Many agencies realized the inadequacy of the brands in this field and transformed into "Social Media Agencies." At the end, this was not something all the brands could have handled within their own body - at least in the beginning. This field required content first and foremost, and then graphics for that content as well as management of the content, CRM and training brands in the field.

Additionally, developing independent applications on Facebook pages specific to corporations became a topic of conversation: Facebook Applications. Software developers were now able to develop applications and games to function within Facebook. These applications increased brand's interaction on its page, strengthen the brand awareness, and enabled agencies to create more extensive projects than social media account management. However, developing applications was a completely different job than managing a readily developed platform's content. This created a separation between the ones who defined themselves as social media account managers of the corporations/brands and app developers; while the first ones were trying to do something like "building management", the second ones were taking on the innovative part of the job. And this blocked the way of marketing the jobs with the real added value directly to the brands.

Today, I observe that the place Facebook occupies in marketing communications is not yet clearly understood. Maybe many marketing media have experienced similar processes and passed through the same problems. However, it is obvious that there are many wrong practices, misguidance as well as social media experts who appeared without even understanding the content of the job and the transformation itself. What I mean by problems is the unparallel between the greed of people and their desire to sell more and the real Facebook communications.

As a matter of fact, posting on Facebook is not to take the ads prepared for conventional media and put them on Facebook as they are. Social media communications doesn't mean to post "Have a good week, happy weekends" on Mondays and Fridays on the brand page. Moreover, Facebook is not even Social Media itself, on the contrary of popular belief!

So, what is it?

QUALITY AND QUANTITY

While everybody in every sector keeps on discussing whether quality or quantity weighs heavier, I say "content" first and foremost in every occasion I get. In other words, we should invest our resources primarily on differentiating our product, brand, service.

Many marketing managers pursue the number of likes on their Facebook pages before they weigh the potential of their own products or brands. Of course I am not saying that the number of likes of the corporate pages is not important; what I am saying is that it is quite absurd for that number to be deceptively high. OK, 1000 is a psychological number as 10,000 is, I understand that. However, the target of 375,000 is not a psychological number. I have known managers who put 375,000 as a target just because their competitor had 375,000 Facebook page likes while they did not have any difference from their equivalents in the market, without having a clue about the spirit of the job. I ask the following questions to those managers:

- What are the differing features of your product?
- What are the different thing you offer to people in terms of content?
- Let us put aside your position in the corporation for a moment. If you didn't have any relation to the corporation and if you were the customer to buy this product, would you really consider your potential as a corporation enough to reach this target group?
- Do you have a marketing plan to reach this number?
- What do you really want: numbers or the truth of this job?
- Would you prefer to establish a sincere relationship with your customers or your potential consumers, or maybe you wouldn't give up the priority of capitalism and its domineering character for anything in the world?

I hope you've noticed that I immediately say goodbye to the ones who are only chasing numbers. However, the marketing managers who want to rise themselves up above the crowd in the eyes of their senior management are obsessed with numbers unfortunately.

It's all very well but surely you haven't gathered 10,000 people on your Facebook page as puppets, have you? You are not collecting numbers there. There are people in the flesh there in front of their computers who liked your page and agreed to communicate with you. These people are in front of their computers and they don't have a tag on their heads indicating Facebook or Twitter follower numbers. They want to be informed about you, to comment on your posts, moreover, to share your joy/sadness. These people want to be close to you. You cannot treat them as simple numbers. You shouldn't!

Yes, Facebook is the strongest social platform now with a viral infrastructure providing WOMM and yes, the best practice of word of mouth marketing could be done here. I haven't seen a better social platform than this which has visual, auditory and textual shares all together as well.

If we are to return to number enthusiasts; you can reach 150,000 people with the word of mouth marketing if we suppose you have 1000 likes on Facebook and this thousand people have 150 friends on average. This means 150,000 people who have a relationship with each other. Maybe now you've started to understand what the ads on the right in Facebook saying "Your friend XXX liked this page" mean. The purpose of these ads is actually this: To reach 750,000 people in the next advertising work by making the like number 5000 just as reaching 150,000 people from 1000 people! So do not underestimate 5000s or 10,000s. If your page has 10,000 likes, this means that you can reach 1,500,000 people from the circles that ten thousand are in and that you have the potential of sending your message to such a large crowd. Of course this potential is for the ones who know how to use it right! I can't help saying this. Social media expert is not a title which is given to the people who understand all of the processes I mentioned above. There is more to it.

You have to use Facebook ads for an organic growth along with managing the fans on your Facebook page. That is why, at the end of the day, your real sales won't reflect the attempts of corporations nor people trying to increase the likes of your page saying "Would you like us to send you 100,000 people bro?" This is what our ancestors called scarcity despite wealth. Everybody knows this quote of Rumi[22]: "Either seem as you are or be as you seem."

The importance of quality and quantity changes

depending on the purposes but at the end of the day, sincerity wins.

FACEBOOK IS NOT FOR FREE

Let's suppose that you have opened a Facebook page for your brand and somehow managed to gather 10,000 people there. Now, you think that everything you say will be received by this 10,000 people and you won't spend a dime for this, don't you? Well, you're wrong. Actually, what is called "Facebook Ads" is a tool related to your Facebook page itself or its content rather than directing people to your website. If your concern is to convey your message to all the people you've gathered in your page, it is impossible to achieve without using ads. At this point, it would be helpful to review the Facebook Share Algorithm we mentioned in the previous chapter once more. At the end, there is a whole mathematics in the background of the matter.

Marketing on Facebook is more measurable and more economic compared to the conventional marketing media but it is absolutely not for free! What I mean here is of course not opening a page or the cost of being on Facebook! Actually, I am not discussing whether using Facebook ads is necessary for a healthy marketing communications strategy or not; I am just talking about its cost.

If you are going to enter to social media somehow and if Facebook is going to be a part of your social media strategy, you absolutely have to have a budget for advertisement. Whether this is $10 daily or $5000 monthly, it doesn't really matter but you should have it as an item on your marketing budgets. Keep this separate from your social media account management budget.

So, what is it again?

It is indispensable to spend money once a Facebook page had been opened.

HOW DOES FACEBOOK NEWS FEED WORK?

Let's say that you haven't used Facebook for one day and as soon as you open Facebook the next day, you've encountered a content that was shared minutes after you've logged out from your Facebook page. In other words, this is old news with regard to Facebook timeline.

A friend has given birth and announced this by putting a picture of the baby. Many people have written comments under it and the picture she shared has received dozens of likes. So why are you seeing this post at the top of your news feed? How does the display algorithm of the news you share on your page work? Here is the formula for you:

$$\sum_{edges\ e} u_e w_e d_e$$

u_e — affinity score between viewing user and edge creator.

w_e — weight of this edge type.

d_e — time decay factor based on how long ago the edge was created.

This formula applies to all page, group and personal posts. Here, there are three main factors determining the weight of a post display on your news feed:

1. How long ago was the post sent.

2. Your relationship/affinity with the person or brand sending the post.
3. How much likes and comments did the content get.

I, therefore, think that especially one item in the above formula will draw marketing people's attention. For the most influential item with which you can intervene to display your message on many people's timeline is Item 3.

This will help us understand the reason for a brand to open ads related to a content that was shared on the page as well. You cannot control people being present in front of the computer at the moment you share the content, neither can you control people's relationship/affinity but you can increase interaction by showing the content via ads and getting more views by doing so.

Facebook will carry the posts which got the likes and comments of the majority to the top, regardless of the first and second items as we've seen on the birth example. That is why brands support a post on their page that they would like to bring forth with ads.

CONTENT/ACCOUNT MANAGEMENT ON FACEBOOK

People who knew MIRC[23] in the early days of Internet would remember; there were virtual personalities who became phenomena in tens of chat rooms. Some of the chat rooms were quite popular. There were frequenters of these chat rooms and every chat room used to be managed by moderators. The ones who were cursing, being naughty or not conforming to the rules of the room were being expelled from the chat room. (Banned.)

The ancestor of Facebook pages is actually MIRC. There was a certain moral sentiment and management style depending on the kind of the chat room in MIRC. Moderators were able to expel you or ban you completely from the chat room if you didn't act accordingly to the rules of the chat room. In short, a totalitarian regime used to prevail in the atmosphere.

This applies to Facebook today as well. The only difference is that MIRC was a closed system and Facebook has a democratic ruling regime in contrast with MIRC. Oh, and we should add the opportunity of limitless sharing to all this.

As much as the place given to you on conventional platform is limited, temporary and has its limits drawn with sharp lines, you are as much limitless, indefinite and free on Facebook on the contrary. This being the case, you have to find group moderators with strong communication skills for your Facebook page who would listen the group, answer their questions, manage disputes arising within the group, answer complaints and calm the troublemakers. This task has to be performed either by a person(s) currently working in your firm whom you believe has the skills to do the job or by a social media agency on behalf of the corporation. Actually the best would be giving the management duty of your Facebook page to people who were trained in-house and who know the language and dynamics of the corporation as I've said before. If you are not able to find suitable people within your corporate body, you need to get support from social media agencies until you've assigned a digital marketing communicator in your firm.

You could be disappointed if you give this duty to inexperienced people only because they have Facebook accounts and use social media actively. This error could swallow up your little excitement about social media completely.

Therefore, first of all, you have to determine a strategy as to the management style of your social media accounts and the places you would be present. You can pay a heavy price for unplanned actions here as you would anywhere else. I should remind once more; you don't have a responsibility with regard to the number of "Likes" on your page. You primarily have a responsibility towards people who came and liked your page. The most fatal error being committed at the beginning is to ignore the fact that the people in flesh sitting in front of their computers could create trouble for you with their comments in the following periods while you target increasing the number of "Likes" on your page.

You have to listen to your crowd, analyze them thoroughly, understand what they like and get to know them very well. Do this especially for the first 200 people who like your page. Yes, you've heard it right. I can say that you would have quite a good sample in order to make generalizations for future when your page reaches to 200 likes.

200 is an important number in deed.

Don't worry; you'll reach that number easily. Even asking your acquaintances, friends, suppliers or employees would be enough.

I graduated from college in 2002. In the third year, reaching to a sample group of 150 in Marketing Research module meant that you could make a very realistic generalization about the subject matter. This meant, in other words, that you could prepare a very extensive and reliable report based on 150 people.

Today you are able to get thousands of answers in just a few hours when you conduct a survey on Facebook. Only this reason is enough for you not to underestimate people who liked your page since this sample group is going to constitute the main core of your crowd which will grow in the future. Later, you will start to look for ways to make the content more attractive for this crowd. As you transform your content into a more attractive one, your number of followers will naturally increase too.

So, now we can proceed to our chapter named "how to increase the number of followers on Facebook in a decent manner?" If you're ready, we will start from scratch.

THE WAYS TO ETHICALLY INCREASE THE NUMBER OF FOLLOWERS ON FACEBOOK

The majority of questions I get during the trainings are related to the ways of increasing the number of people in Facebook pages. First of all, I want to repeat a sentence I tell everyone here as well for you: "100 real page followers are better than neither fish nor fowl 10,000 bought with money." I listed the things you should do with this manifesto step by step below.

Even though the explanations may seem to be mainly about Facebook, it actually contains recommendations applicable to other social networks as well.

1. Create Your Page and Start Inviting

Once you've created your page in the related category and product group, start inviting your friends to like your page. When you reach to 25 likes - this can change later - you will be able to identify your page with a name under the domain name Facebook. e.g. http://facebook.com/yazarsalihseckinsevinc. You can access this feature from the administration section of your page.

You can get all the detailed information related to how to do this by searching it on Facebook Help. The link addresses of Facebook Help may change in time but Facebook will always have a Help Center for sure. I want you to promise something in case you encounter an obstacle: Google the question you're asking!

Proceed?

Send invites to your friends, acquaintances, employees by special messages asking them to like your page. It wouldn't hurt at all to ask this directly! You can assure them that their liking the page would contribute a lot to your marketing activities in the future. Thus come 150 people...

I probably don't need to say to you that you are not obliged to send all the invites only through Facebook. You can invite people by e-mails you will send via your website, your corporation, by business cards, by your brochures, by phone; in short you can use all the materials and tools you use to communicate and contact people on behalf of your corporation to invite people.

Go to them with a reasonable suggestion phrase for them to like you. If you serve as an independent vehicle workshop repairing Toyota brand vehicles, for example, you can say "Like our page and contact us if you have any question." Or if you are selling mobile phones and accessories phrases such as "Like our Facebook page, stay updated about constantly changing mobile phone world!" would work. "As you can see, we know what we are talking about. Our offers are on matters we specialize on. We trust our expertise to guide us."

Way to go; now you gathered 250 people easily...

2. Let the Ads Begin

Actually, 100 people would be enough. We will begin advertising with this crowd. I can hear you say "OK but where to place the ad?" We will place the ad on our Facebook page we've created for our brand. Have you forgotten? We will reach 15,000 people from the environment of 100 people on Facebook through their 150 friends on average. Facebook lets you do this. We will take out an ad such as "Your friend XX liked this page" to invoke those 15,000 people's curiosity and make more people like our page by doing so. You can always see "Help" section to get informed about Facebook ads and how to place them. Once you've selected the page like news from sponsored news and determined your daily budget ($10-$20, it doesn't matter) you will have your ad placed for 15,000 people to see and made your first wave move to make people like your page. This way, you will have 800-1000 people who liked your page in approximately one week. On top of it, the friends of your friends who are within your first degree circle will already like your page. So, congratulations. You have created your core audience. Now, you really have a community to manage.

We have already discussed the blog experience. I mean the blogs which are your main base and in which everybody is a publisher and can create content. Now it is time for you to show your skills that you've developed there on your Facebook page.

3. Start Listening and Continue Listening

If fifty percent of the communication is talking, the other fifty percent is listening. In fact, listening is considered to have more percentage than that in a healthy communication. I've treated both equally. That is why I said fifty percent. Still, you should remember that listening weighs heavier in communication.

You have to listen in the whole world of Internet and not just in Facebook. This way, you will be able to understand what is being said about your brand and how you are perceived from outside more clearly and determine how to act according to that quickly. What you should do for this is pretty easy on Facebook. To make a search of your brand name or the word or word group you want to find on Facebook Search. You will feel really lucky when you do the same on Google as well.

The process of listening should be a permanent part of your communication and should stay in the cycle constantly. To understand what matters to people will help you to approach them in a more correct and healthy tone. I suppose we all want to understand what our customers really desire and act upon it.

Only be careful! I am not saying you should follow. I am saying you should listen. Listen to what is being talked about you. You can get involved with the dialogue by answering the comments on your page but please just listen when you are to listen without answering. "Following" is a little more Terminatoresque term. Inanimate objects and posts would be followed. Therefore, I deem the word "listening" more suitable here since it is more humane. Many marketing professionals also take great care to use this term in social media and say "listening". Because the term "listening" is more humane.

There are paid or free methods to listen what is being talked about in social media. I just need to Google it if you want to learn more. In short, Google Alerts, Twitter Search, Facebook Search, Youtube Search will do the job for you.

Additionally, if you want to see the firms who are giving paid professional listening services with detailed analyses, I would recommend you to check out Monitera and Somedya.

4. Be Sincere, Real and Transparent

Sincerity is one of the most important indicators of social media. Here, sincerity doesn't only mean honesty. You have to get rid of your corporate jargon as well. Mission, vision, purpose... These are the business subject matters of ten years ago. Don't be snob, for example, if your brand doesn't require you to be. For that matter, getting a little away from the corporate talk will work for you. It is difficult, isn't it? Don't huff and puff, you can do it! The emails I get address me as "Mr. Salih" but I would not feel uncomfortable at all when a Facebook page I like addresses me directly with my first name. Addressing attitudes are very different on Facebook from what we are used to. People are on Facebook primarily for fun. (There are other platforms for "Ladies and gentlemen", we will be talking about these social platforms in the following pages.)

At the end, the unrealistic call center dialogues, customer service calls which do not help at all but always end with "Is there anything I can help you with?", the liar salesmen who pass beyond cringing and who seem to be thinking your benefit but actually only care about your money, the phone calls you cannot be sure whether you are talking to a human or a robot, the brands which are trying surprise us and imprint their products on our brains when we open the newspaper... Social Media is a more "humane" communication platform which eliminates all these communication processes which have been dictated to us but which we could never get used to.

You, also, can be more of a big brother, friend, baby brother or uncle there. Develop a sincere style for your posts and just enjoy this.

Won't you make any mistakes? Of course you will. We are only human at the end. However, you can correct a misunderstanding quickly if you understand where you went wrong and apologize. Don't be afraid of making a mistake on social media.Be afraid of acting like a robot. Apologizing is something very humane. If you are one of those who say "We don't apologize" and if social media is a part of your job, I can say that you will be in a lot of trouble.

So long as you act sincerely, realistic and humane in your communications, your customers will trust you, will be shopping from you and most importantly will share your posts with their friends.

5. Think as a Consumer

Do you like watching TV ads? Or maybe I should rephrase my question: how much do you enjoy the pop-up ads you encounter when you are searching for something on the Internet? Do you start to feel nauseated immediately once your phone rings in the middle of a very important job and you hear "Hi Mr. Salih, first of all, our conversation will be recorded due to security reasons"? If you say you enjoy this that could indicate a pathological problem in you unless you are an adman or related to the sector. Frankly, I have never seen anybody who liked these things.

Unfortunately, none of us like these types of things but we all commit the same mistake when it comes to our own product's sales and marketing.

Just think of all the materials pouring down on us everyday from the brands...
- Direct mails
- Magazine ads
- TV ads
- Radio ads
- Promotional packages
- Brochures slipped into our hands while walking on the street
- Billboards
- Advertisements you are subjected to about new products of a brand while you are waiting on the phone to get something done
- SMSes
- 20 minutes long ads you have to watch in theatres
- E-mails coming to your mailbox even though you have never visited the mentioned website
- The sales and marketing calls coming to your office or cell phones

Just put yourself into your customer's shoes. I know, it is easier said than done. Nonetheless, you would admit that the list above contains irritating and undesired things for the majority of people.

For the ones who ask "Well, what should we do, not

try to sell our product at all?" I would answer by saying that social media exists right at this point in order to relieve those irritating processes. Facebook provides you with the most suitable foundation for this. If you trust your product, it will be enough for you to make it ready for purchasing. Let people market your product for you. Every individual actually opens an account on Facebook to have fun, to communicate with their loved ones and spend an enjoyable time. And if you can meet them right on this ground at this point, that means you are on the right track.

For example, I would absolutely recommend you to look at the fun shares of JeansLab on social media related to country's agenda. They add humor and they create a viral effect everybody can use by producing shareable content on Facebook.

If we return back to the matter of thinking as your customers, please ask yourself the below questions for every Facebook message you send and for all the content you share:
- Is the content I am going to share a forced content created just for the sake of posting something? In other words, would people who will get this message really benefit from it or really like it?

Would I want to receive such content as a consumer?

If the answer to both of the questions is "Yes", you are on the right track.

6. Answer Both Negative and Positive Comments

Don't leave positive comments unanswered. I see this frequently. A share has been made, people liked it. In other words, it is treated as a fait accompli. Yet it is not so! Not answering people who are saying nice things about you clearly translates as "I am not listening to you". You would be loosing that person's interest for your next post. Just think about it; you have complimented someone and they haven't even bothered to answer you. After this, why would you be interested in posts of someone who didn't even show the decency to answer you? OK, let's say you cannot even say thank you, but the least you can do is to use the "Like" buttons Facebook has placed under the comments. What would happen if you clicked on it once? Would your finger fall off?

People would like to know that you are communicating with them.

There is another matter quite opposite of this. You have to answer negative comments as well. Let's suppose that you have shared something and got a negative comment about this post. Moreover, you've been careless enough to delete that negative comment. Oh good heavens! You've made the mistake of the century. This is the same thing with someone giving you a complaint letter and you reading it and then ripping it up and throwing the pieces to their face. In other words, it is the impolite way of saying "I don't care about you at all". Social media is too social to tolerate this kind of actions.

Just watch what happens after this; this man goes and creates a group called "The Ones Who Hate XXX Brand" on Facebook, starts a campaign tagged #gotohellxxx on Twitter. He shares photos you would never want to see next to your brand on Facebook and tags your brand on this photo together with 500 people on his friends list. Moreover, he starts smear campaigns under this photo saying "XXX Brand Did This to Me, Come On, Join Me and Let's Teach These Impudent People a Lesson!" Later you are in a pretty scrape. One minute to another you would be confronting a serious social media crisis.

The correct attitude here would be to say to the negative commenter that you are looking into the matter, that you are investigating it and that you would be contacting him directly with a message as soon as you have a conclusive answer right under the negative comment he left. Now you've lofted the ball. Later, you would really need to take action on this matter. Otherwise, you would go back to the beginning and this time the flames would be more embittered than ever, I promise you.

In other words, if we are to summarize the moves you should make, first return the coming ball with your chest. Soften it a little, and then let it to your foot. At last the control and the responsibility is all yours. Then, make your move towards goal and invite the opposing team's player to have a dinner together after the match. I know that it isn't that easy and need mastering. Yet this is the most correct thing to do.

7. Interact with People

You will hear a lot of this word: interaction.

This is the thing of social media: the interaction which started with Web 2.0, in other words the interaction which came together with the second period of Internet and its evolution. Interaction tells you this in short: "Do not stay passive. This media is not like what it is used to be. Do not withdraw after saying what you have to say. Tell people something that they can talk about, that they can discuss. Make them talk. Develop content that will make them talk. Answer their questions. Provide content that will benefit them. Share your expertise. Let them ask questions. Ask them to create content for you. Enable people who like your page interact with each other too. In short, keep your community sober. All the systems which contain monotone, boring, standard content are doomed to be destroyed in such a dynamic platform.

However I would like to say one more thing; do not exaggerate. Don't worry; you will know and feel when to stop. Your followers will lead you to the right communication model. You will shape them and they will shape you. You will start to understand better what works and what doesn't in time as long as you interpret your data correctly. You will walk on the path of your brand perception and your discourse at the end and get feedback from people in this direction as well.

8. Organize Mini Campaigns

Not too extensive but mini campaigns. Campaigns with little gifts at the end. More like campaigns that would make the people who have already liked your page feel privileged. Think of it as a sort of thank you for liking you.

You will be organizing modest campaigns for their choice of being in communication with you by liking your page. That is all. But be careful; many corporation make the same mistake. Don't think about creating big projections with little campaign designs. It will backlash. You may think of organizing big ones too but this depends on your budget of course. I will talk about this in detail in the next chapter.

The content might include: Prize questions, prize questionnaires, and works to be created by your followers and evaluated by them again... Your imagination is your limit in creating original and independent mini projects specific to each brand.

This kind of mini campaigns would make your page more attractive. Some of the campaigns may be aimed at increasing the number of followers while some could be organized just for the people who liked your page feel privileged. Their design is completely up to you. This type of little fun events would maximize the interaction on your page as long as they are in the right dosage and do not create disturbance.

9. Organize Big Campaigns, Develop Applications

If you have a decent marketing budget, you can work miracles. You can contact digital agencies which have a creative team and order Facebook games or apps to be made on your behalf; you can put your signature under visually strong and extensive projects with higher quality; of course by offering bigger carrots at the end. Fully open the taps since you've already turned them on. You may not even need to offer a carrot for every production you make depending on from where the winds of ideas are blowing.

If you create a game to be integrated into your page, don't forget that it will be your developed product. If you create a good game, everybody who likes your page would continue to play it even if your campaign period is over. Every app and game you develop is actually an excuse for people to spend more time on your page and talk more about you. This way your contact surface with people on social media would grow and this would reveal you innovative side as well. The best example of this can be seen in Redbull. They are keeping people on platforms that would make people talk about them more and keep them busy with games, apps, Internet radios, Internet TVs, mobile apps and many more.

Another great example is the incredible success achieved by Tripadvisor which has seen an independent Facebook app developer's success of "Where I Have Been" app and quickly developed "Cities I've Visited" app. Today "Cities I've Visited" Facebook app has more than 5,000,000 monthly active users. People mark places they have been and places they want to go on Google Map. I suppose I don't need to mention the power a tourism firm gets from this information.

The fact that the person who has developed "Where I Have Been" app (Craig Ulliot) has an established tourism firm today which may not be as big as Tripadvisor, is nothing other than a great example for the potential a little app has.

Although it may not be as big a success as Tripadvisor's but the Bung the Dragon game we developed (as Daha-Baska) for McCannErickson Azerbaijan is still being played by 300-500 people on average monthly and continues to attract new fans to McCann Erickson Azerbaijan's Facebook page.

Note: McCann Erickson had newly created its page on Facebook when we developed the game.

10. Create Value

It is very comfortable for social media people to share the content searched on different sources and found. But a certain content always has a certain cycle. It would be consumed and finished. Well, what will we be sharing if no content is produced? We have to think about that too.

There is no reason for you to hide that you are an opinion leader on the subjects you are expert of. But you have to spend more effort to transform this into content. You have probably struggled a lot to express yourself about the field you are an expert of in a little column on a newspaper before. Here is a limitless area for you. Be sure that someone is going to read your content and remember you, maybe even want to contact you. Producing useful content about your job, writing articles, shooting videos; all of this means more reliability, recognition and sales. You will be gaining reliability and recognition as much as you produce high quality content and share them.

If you are an accountant, for example, and prepare and share an article titled "10 Things you need to know about the New Commercial Code", be assured that there will be many people to benefit from this and you will also be laying foundations for the potential customers who want to work with you because of your expertise. In other words, you won't be trying to sell your services forcefully; you will rather be transforming it into valuable content and facilitating your services to be purchased by your customers.

You can also use the content you've produced for your blog on Facebook.

If you are not able to write for pages, keep your writings short. Additionally, remember that you have three different options to publish on the Internet: video, text and audio. One of them surely is right for you. I can also say that writing is something you get better at in time by working on it as everything else is. I used to write so bad back in the old days that my boss wanted me to send every e-mail I write to him first and then send it to the customer once it has been approved. I can admit that I feel ashamed when I turn back two years later and read the first texts I've written on Harbiyiyorum.com. However, everything gets better once you spend time on it. Come to think of it, I got so courageous about it that I intended to write a book.

As you create content in the fields of your expertise, people will have an idea about you even though they do not read your texts and you will be the first to come to their minds once they want to purchase the product or service you are offering. When the need to purchase the product or service you offer arises, there will be no need for the people to do research about the matter since you have already had provided the atmosphere of trust with the shares you've done with all your sincerity in the field of your expertise.

A lawyer friend of mine shared an informing post the other day about how to get back the account maintenance fee banks are charging from us on Facebook. I read and shared it on my profile. People, who read it from my profile and liked it, shared it on their own profiles. The ones who read and shared that post now know which lawyer to contact when a need in the field of business law arises.

The age is the age of sincerely sharing the things you know and your expertise. My father will get very angry when he hears this!

11. Carrying on with the Ads

Yes, we've done some ad work in the beginning and left it there. Do you think we are going to do with that? Of course not. Come on, cough it up. Now, as some things fell into place and you've started to see some favorable results, you can carry on with the Facebook ads in order to increase the number of your followers. Furthermore, perpetually this time.

Set a budget and proceed. You will always need ads in order to organically multiply the number of your followers you increased through campaigns. Additionally, you will have to show questionnaires, questions, important developments etc. that you share on your page to a specific audience via ads, apart from the page like ad. You will understand the functioning and benefits of Facebook ads better as you use them and open ads in different combinations.

When the number of your followers is 50,000, not all the contents you post on your page will be seen by 50,000 people (see previous chapter's How Does Facebook News Feed Work? part.) You will use ads in order to reach the people who liked your page but couldn't see the content you've put on your page at the moment of share.

When you start a campaign, you will necessarily need ads to show that campaign to the related target groups. I listed various combinations to open an ad below.

You can open an ad according to following combinations:

1. Page like ad (To the friends of the people who liked your page)
2. Page like ad (To everybody or a specific audience)
3. Ad for page post (e.g. to everybody who liked the page about the questionnaire)
4. Ad for page post (e.g. to everybody who liked the page about the questionnaire)
5. Ad for page post (to the friends of the people who liked the page about the campaign content)

It would be useful for you to try one or two of these combinations at a time. You can also try all of them at one and the same time.

If social media is going to play a part in your digital marketing strategy and if you're planning to develop this area in line with a strategy, Facebook ads must definitely be in this strategy! I will be talking more in detail about Facebook ads in the following chapters.

No need to thank me Mr. Mark Zuckerberg.

12. Do Not Try to Sell Anything, Just Prepare People for Purchasing

You are already doing direct marketing on your website, conventional advertisement media and your classical marketing materials. This would be too much irritating in social media and would backlash. First of all, it is against its nature. You have to communicate with people here and don't forget that communication is reciprocal.

Your seeing a product a friend of yours bought over the Internet on the Facebook news feed, is the best of word of mouth marketing. Firstly, this means that your friend has already bought that product. Secondly, there are no messages saying you should buy it. Even though you don't need that product at that time, believe me, that product will be the first thing to come to your mind when the time comes.

If you want to learn more about subconscious marketing, I recommend you to read Martin Lindstrom's book named Buyology.

There is no harm in repeating: the most effective method of marketing is through the things we hear from our friends, family and acquaintances and their recommendations. Facebook is the most suitable platform for this with a viral infrastructure to make this process function.

What you need to do is to adapt your existing sales channels to social media. Moreover, make your products purchasable through Facebook, if possible. For people do not want to leave Facebook. Do not try to make sales on social media with an aggressive attitude; rather make your products purchasable and available on social media. This way you would be transforming your social media channels into social sales channels.

It is a known thing now that some e-commerce platforms open stores in Facebook pages. This sounds quite reasonable. Who would even consider opening a store in a regular street of a regular neighborhood while there is the opportunity to open a store on 5th Avenue, NYC?

Still, one has to remember that people are on Facebook primarily to communicate, to socialize and to have fun. You must develop your current strategies considering this fact. You must make your sales operations simple, fun and sharable as much as possible. Additionally, you must never pressure people. For this, of course it is a must to thoroughly understand which archetypes social platforms are based on.

Do not forget that sales and marketing are undesirable and negatively perceived concept for the most part. People don't desire something to be sold or marketed to them. Building entrances in our country have the writing on them that says "Salesmen Are Not Allowed!" This is a preconception which is very hard to overcome even today.

Yet, people like to choose and buy the things they need themselves. The mastery is in the ability to do this without disturbing the other party. It is even enough for you to be in sight for your sales to increase. This way, your reputation and recognition level would get higher. And this comes to mean new sales. Social media provides you with this.

If you can correctly understand the 12 items I've mentioned above, you would also understand that these are not applicable just to Facebook. The things I've mentioned are valid and essential things for all the strategies you would design by using social media in digital marketing communications. This list may be expanded but the most important of all is to understand the essence of the matter.

Marketing communications evolves with social media today. One must thoroughly understand how this happens, when it started and which ground it is laid upon before taking any action.

CHRONIC WRONG PRACTICES IN THE SECTOR

If I were to round up main problems I encounter at many corporations I consulted and analyzed Facebook content management of, I can say the following:
1. Social media agencies are, for the most part, agencies which use the already existing content rather than creating content. Therefore, what is expected from social media agencies and what they actually offer do not generally correspond to each other. A corporation has to have a really strong marketing budget and strategy along with correctly founded brand content based on this strategy in order to overcome this handicap.
The original content related to the brand/product must be provided through other channels as well and should be designed by creative agencies taking into account their use on social media specifically.

I remember using the following words in a conference: "Develop games on Facebook, order applications to be written, conduct quality campaigns, seek for the ways to integrate social media to mobile tech and try to integrate social media to real life by doing all this. If you don't do these things, and moreover if you cannot budget ads on Facebook, do not expect much from the social medium Facebook provides."
2. All the brands must get rid of the paradigm of "Have a happy week" and "We wish all the people who like our page a happy weekend" that is being practiced at the beginning and at the end of the week right away. Of course there is no harm in saying "Hello" now and again but when it is automated like this, it starts to become meaningless.
3. It is also important to give up saying "Good morning" everyday and "Good night" every evening.
4. Facebook may be the platform on which scoring points from dead people is being abused the most. What Onur Air did right after the earthquake in Van[24] was wrong but it was equally wrong for many brand pages to express their condolences upon the death of a very famous theatre actor and turn this into content which would create interaction.
5. Forget sharing links from your website on your Facebook page constantly!
6. Do not delete negative comments. Show people that you respond to negative comments as well and that you have an attitude tending to solve the problems.
7. Please avoid sharing low quality and silly pictures you find here and there as well.
8. Corporations request social media agencies to constantly share content. They create an atmosphere as if the agencies do not deserve the money they get when

there is no share. Therefore, the number of meaningless shares on page increases. Every corporation has to have a share cycle reasonable for their own sector. According to a research, more than 15 shares a month starts to create disturbance for people. For some corporations, even two posts a week could be considered too much.

9. If you share three posts in one hour, you could be branded as a SPAMMER and loose some of your followers. Time is precious for everybody. (I've left many pages I liked just because of this.)

10. Avoid sharing things you've prepared with the understanding of conventional advertisement media, dictating your product to people. For this might not always work on Facebook. If you are going to share something which was prepared for conventional media, I recommend you do this by attaching an explanatory cover letter which rephrases it for your Facebook fans.

11. The high number of campaigns would in time start to create the same effect as saying "Hello" or "Good evening" everyday. I am not saying that you shouldn't conduct any campaign. However, do not exaggerate it! Later on, you would start to disappoint other followers of yours who have different expectations from you while being busy with an audacious, campaign freak crowd.

In short, keep it moderate. "Enough" is as good as a feast!
More on misunderstandings

There is an article I wrote on SMN (Sosyal Medya Nedir. net) at the end of 2011 titled "10 Things Firms Get Wrong about Social Media" about malpractices on Facebook and misunderstandings and wrong implementations on Social Media in general. You can consider this article as a summary of what I've been telling in order to clearly draw the frame of the subjects discussed in previous chapters.

10 THINGS FIRMS GET WRONG ABOUT SOCIAL MEDIA

I constantly encounter misunderstandings of "Social Media" at many firms I consult. No matter how hard I try to explain this to my customers, this process is getting even more difficult due to the deficiencies in the dimensions of marketing communications and strategy as well as wrong approaches to the matter. I have listed wrong approaches below and put my comments under them.

1. "Social Media" is enough to promote the firm all by itself.

For some reason, the economic budgets of social media areas compared to classical advertisement media must be responsible for this perception. There is no such thing.

2. Facebook and Twitter are "Social Media" themselves.

Sure. Let's see you trying to be only at those places. Just have a little fun; and see how daddy Google kicks you around at the end of the year.

3. It is enough for me just to make my announcements, inform people about my newly launched products and my corporation on Facebook and Twitter.

Uh-huh. Yes. You have many friends around you who are always dying for your stories right? Let your ego aside and just think about when was the last time you've seen those friends. You keep on talking about yourself all the time, just like this. Don't ask them how they are doing. Don't create content people will be interested in or develop applications and just turn your nose up at the quality projects. Be assured that it will work.

4. I want a hundred million likes just as our competitors. I want it now. Look how people are flying high. We are still at eight thousands.

Yes. How nice. You should first think about how you will manage that eight thousand people as well as the other nine hundred thousand people you reach through their circles and how you can create an interaction with such an audience. Just respond decently to the questions of these people first. If you want numbers, numbers are already everywhere. And those likes wouldn't be worth a dime if you don't have a team able to manage the audience when your crowd becomes ten thousand. This is the most erroneous attitude of all.

5. We will be launching a new service one week later. We want this to be announced on social media. We need this urgently. Let's reach everyone on the Internet. We expect a big return from social media this time.

Sure. That is the only purpose of the existence of social media anyway. Your followers are dying to hear the news of your new service about which even you have just learned today. You gather people around and always make them announcements of your new products. Believe me; you will get an incredible return just by making announcements.

6. I can reach masses very quickly by using social media.

Yes and no. It depends on where you are looking from. However, I usually answer firms with "No". To tell the truth, social networks enable you to establish a two-way communication with communities. It is a long-term investment. It is a marathon. How happy are the firms which are able to manage their communities nicely in an original and non-manipulated way and establish nice dialogues and create values with their content.

7. Everything I publish on Facebook could be seen by the people who like my page.

There is no such thing. Fortunately, there is a formula of this. You can think of the content that falls on your Facebook news feed as the e-mails you receive in your mailbox and in this case, the ones you've never opened/you haven't been interested in don't come to your mailbox again. It wouldn't matter even if you have one billion people in your community unless you create interaction. They wouldn't be informed about you or the content you post.

8. I have a high number of followers, that's great.

Just sit there and break into tears. Your actual work begins now. Content, implementation, movement, interaction, action... You have to fulfill all these requirements. Expand your team. Find a CRM person. Create idea teams. Seek support. There are many social media people on the market (Facebook people, Twitter people). There isn't any marketing communicator!

9. Group purchasing websites are also social media actually.

Now, right at this point, we understand how high the level of confusion is. The customer actually tries to say this: For me, social media is the whole body of opportunities of marketing communications and sales channels on the Internet. Wrong but there is something right as well looking from the perspective of the customer. For everybody is trying to earn their bread at the end of the day.

10. Facebook ads do not work.
Very good. Continue in this direction!

More on Facebook ads

You can place an ad on a page on Facebook, an announcement you share on the page or a website of your liking independently of your page on Facebook and the number of your fans. You can open your ad directed at certain categories such as country, city, age, gender, marital status etc. as well as show it according to certain interests and to Facebook users who have more specific qualities.

The list of features to narrow down the ad audience is ever-lengthening: firms, sectors, people who got engaged in the last 6 months, people who got married in the last 6 months, people who moved to a new house, people who changed the cities they live in, hobbies, people who live away from their families, people who have a new born baby, golf players, mobile phone owners etc.

Let's assume that you've developed a mobile app for iPhone and iPad. You can give an ad directly at the address of this app on iTunes. In other words, the people who are going to see your ad will be the people who have iPhones and iPads and interested in iOS. To do this, it would be enough for you to narrow down your target group based on country and age on Facebook Ads page according to the content of your app and mark users who like iPhone and iPad page in the category of technology. For instance, we direct our advertisement works specifically to this category when we launch our mobile (iOS) apps since iPhone and iPad users constitute the audience we are aiming at directly.

Here is another example; let's say that you are going to announce a Justine Bieber concert. You can target Justin Bieber fans directly in this case or you can show this ad to the fans of artists of similar style such as Katy Perry, Justin Timberlake, One Direction etc. as well.

If you sell products such as push chair, feeding chair etc., newly weds and the ones who just gave birth constitute your very audience, if you ask me. If you sell kitchen appliances, you can show your ad to food & beverage fans on Facebook, members of gourmet pages and even the ones who like Zagat.com.

In short, it is hard to underestimate the power of Facebook ads. It is also possible to create ads for everybody in a way to give results for every budget. What is important here is for you to know your audience well.

TWITTER

Twitter is our one and only site created through the marriage of SMS and MSN after Web 2.0 with the addition of a little social media spirit. Before that, we used to chat with our friends on MSN and these chats were private. Now, we follow who says what to whom, what people are talking about, what the most popular subject is on Twitter. Additionally, Twitter limits the number of character of the texts we share similarly to SMS, and enables us to cut the long story short and share brief and to the point texts.

Of course, what we are looking for is not limited to that. As always, we seek to use this medium too for our marketing activities with the thought of money being where the people are. Some others, on the other hand, are after popularity. Some of us are still trying to understand what it is. I use Twitter as a diary for notes to myself.

Whatever it is, Twitter has positioned itself as the most popular social medium following Facebook and it will probably stay there for a long time. This is why it became a very important medium for all the marketing people. Additionally, the word "to tweet" has already taken its place within verbs just like to Google.

It is crucial to understand the correct usage of Twitter in marketing communications as it is everywhere else. Of course, quality and quantity come to the fore here as well. Having more followers doesn't mean that you are conducting a correct marketing communications strategy (as it is on Facebook). Follower is something you can easily buy on Twitter. People new in the sector and want to show their professionalism in this area are trying to be popular by buying themselves followers. They think: Many followers show that you are famous.

Yet, as a marketing expert, there is another thing about Twitter that excites me more than posting tweets or finding followers. I will share this with you too. I can even say that Twitter is the medium that excites me the most within all the other social media just because of this feature.

During the college years, we were taught about the "4Ps of Marketing" in the Marketing module. These were: Product, Price, Place, and Promotion. (We can list many of those Ps.) In other words, you would be structuring a perfect marketing operation if you could bring together these four factors in the most effective way possible. Yet, actually doing that was an utopia. This perfect quartet has always stayed on my mind as a cloud. Just think about this: bringing these four factors together in the optimum way. Moreover, doing so without adding other variables into the equation. It is very difficult. Even impossible.

When I discovered this feature of Twitter, the 4 Ps of Marketing stopped being a cloud in my mind and I understood the concept more clearly.

Some of my friends surprisingly can say such things when critiquing Twitter: "What is the point in letting people know what I will cook for dinner or which bay I am hanging out for holiday? Who would even want to know that?" At first, I also thought that it was pointless, posting tweets even when going to the bathroom seemed absurd to me. However, believe me that now I am interested in this more than everything in my business life. This feature of Twitter is much more important than how many followers people have, how many tweets they are posting and how many retweets they are getting.

On Twitter, people tell you what they are doing, what they want, and what kind of mood they are in straightforwardly. Ye marketing fellows? Does this ring a bell for you? Moreover, they do this as in their own way and without hiding anything from anybody. They know that they are being peeped at and they tell so. This way, we are establishing two of the 4Ps of marketing already. (Place, Promotion). Besides, it is simultaneous. Could there be a better thing for a marketing professional than this?

So, how do we do this? In other words, how do we see what people are talking about and what they want?

Twitter Search

Months ago, just as I completed a post I wrote for Harbiyiyorum.com and was looking for different ways to share it on Twitter, I discovered "Twitter Search". I thought "Hold up, let's see what I can search here" Just as I was thinking that this was not something related to searching help content on Twitter, I wrote "I'm hungry" to the search field and waited for the results to show up. In a few seconds tens of tweets lined up on the phone's screen. Tweets were as below in general:

"I'm dying of hunger."

"Can somebody throw a toast on my face? I am very hungry."

"My mom is not at home and I am very hungry."

"Ugh I am sooo hungry, somebody buy me a burger =)"

"I should write it here as well. I am hungry, do you get it, hungry!"

"I am a hungry man!"

This being the case, I started to search for words such as "food", "cheese", "olive", "kebab", "doner" etc. The result was really surprising. People were telling they got hungry and tweeting what they were eating at every moment and this was whetting my appetite to answer them in my field of expertise. Moreover, new tweets with the same word were coming as I was trying to write an answer for each tweet and the stream was constantly being updated.

You cannot even imagine how the number of tweets containing the word "hungry" increases especially during the late hours of the night and in the noon time. I can only explain this with one sentence: I had found my entertainment.

To the one asking someone to buy him a burger, I was posting "Here you are, not the burger itself but it may inspire you a little. I hope you can really eat your burger as soon as possible" and giving the link to the category burgers were at my website while promoting @harbiyiyorum's Twitter account. I started promoting my website this way.

The one question I had in my mind was whether I would get reaction or not by answering tweets of people I don't know at all. I answered hundreds of people to date. Moreover, about a sensitive subject and to the point of provoking people who were saying that they were "hungry". Yet, not a soul stepped up and said "Who are you bro? Why are you sending me messages?" Many of them even thanked me. Some of them said "I am adding this website to my RSS list after preliminary review". Some of them said "It is a great website, fantastic foods". And some "Retweeted" the answer I wrote to them. In short, they became familiar with Harbiyiyorum.com, promoted my website to their own followers, and interacted with me and as a result, my website's traffic increased. People I answered started following me on Twitter.

There is no SPAM here if you don't exaggerate things. No pressure. A need arises for an individual and you offer a useful bit of information for the one requesting it at that moment. Is there anything more beautiful than this for a marketing professional?

Finally, I understood that Twitter was already a place on which people are open to peeping at each other and sending messages to each other comfortably and the strongest weapon of Twitter was actually Twitter Search..

How can I use Twitter Search?

You are not limited with the keywords related to your field on Twitter Search. You can, for example, search to see what people are talking about your brand. I already mentioned this within the social media following tools previously. You can respond to the people writing positively or negatively about you and the people with complaints and you can structure a unique and proactive customer services for them.

Besides, if we are to consider that people are going to get used to this proactivity, you immediately have to get rid of your habit of not listening anything that is being said about you after you've experienced a misfortune.

Let's suppose that you own a web store selling souvenirs. The words you will search for could be listed as "gift", "present", "birthday" but if you ask me, you must also include certain special occasions and special weeks. You will encounter tweets such as below probably:

"It is my mom's birthday and I don't know what to give her as a gift." "Somebody give me a chess board as a gift."
"Ugh, what should I buy as a present?"

Well, what you should do is obvious in this case. People are directly telling you that they are looking for a gift and asking you to help them. What else do you want? Now all you have to do is to say "How can I help you?" and guide your potential customer.

There is a point, however, to be careful about. You should know that the effect of the answer you give using your corporation's Twitter account and your own personal account will differ when you answer people over Twitter Search. As I repeated time and again before, do not, in any circumstance, try to sell anything to anybody here as well. The accomplishment is always subject to compliment. Talk to people in such a way to make them compliment you. This way your skills will turn into accomplishment. And your sales will increase.

Although the power of Twitter Search is not completely understood in Turkey yet, I would like to share two incidents I've experienced.

I went on a business trip to Ankara last December. I was going to go by bus. I tweeted "Let the journey to Ankara begin" on my Twitter account. 5 minutes later, a friend of mine answered me with "Bon voyage". Approximately 1 hour after this conversation, I got a tweet from Pamukkale Tourism's Twitter account I have never followed before saying "Traveling is freedom. We wish you a happy journey." It was a very professional and well-thought sentence. Pamukkale Tourism was not trying to sell me anything and it was not also a self-promoting message. The message was quite clear. They have written a message directed at my mood and the context I was in directly and this message won my heart. I, immediately, wrote back to them. They answered me with the same speed. So, a dialogue has begun between us.

I was traveling with another bus firm at that time. I cannot express how surprised and excited I got when I received that message. Just think about the number of people posting tweets everyday on "Journey" and "Travel". It is obvious that Pamukkale Tourism conducts a serious work here.

So, do you think that Pamukkale Turizm is successful? They did not sell me anything directly. They did not slander the bus firm I was traveling with. They did not offer me a coupon and said "try us next time". Yet, I am sure that you can guess which bus firm I will prefer for my next bus journey.

To top it all, I was so touched that I told this incident as an example in my book. That is to say they have been successful.

Similarly, we made a visit to Azerbaijan at the end of 2011 for business purposes. We went to a venue named Otto which was a very popular hot spot in Baku. Everybody was smoking inside since there was no ban on smoking. As I was almost poisoned to death due to the smoke, I reached out for Twitter and wrote "Baku is beautiful. Otto is a nice place but I cannot take this smoke anymore." I got a tweet from an account named @sicakbahce in response saying "It could have been very different if it was us ;)". I immediately went to their website to see. It was an innovative company which transformed the outdoor heating devices into tables. I didn't ask but they got me probably from the word "smoke". It was still astonishing for them to start a conversation with me in this way. OK, so then what happened? I reported the approach of this company which has nothing to do with me or my job to a friend of mine who owns a café exactly as a case. I don't know if my friend ever shopped from them later but I am sure "Sicak Bahce" is making great sales by doing so.

Do not try to sell anything on Twitter. Just get involved in the conversation.

Are you an organization teaching German language? Just search for "speak German" and see what comes up. For a firm selling energy drink, bottled water or any kind of soft drink, the word "thirsty" is an opportunity for you to communicate with people. 15 people wrote that they are thirsty, for example, in the last one hour as of this moment. And try searching "thirsty" in the summer season.

Twitter Search is a formidably unique tool in the field of marketing communications today. I say this in every conference and training with a strong emphasis and every time I shudder a little with the awareness of the experience of witnessing this.

The first thing that comes to my mind when the subject is marketing in social media is "Twitter Search". Anyhow, you must have understood by now that "Twitter Search" requires a hard work. And this equalizes competition for all corporations.

I won't be giving information such as how to increase number of followers on Twitter or how to create an effective hashtag in this book. There are people who are better than me in doing so after all. As a marketing professional, the real-time interaction with people on Twitter is more than enough for me.

The only thing I can say to you about increasing the number of followers is this: your number of followers will increase anyway as long as you are sincere and interact with people.

Sometimes I see job applications bragging about how much Twitter followers they have or how much Retweet they get. Believe me; we are not even a bit interested in follower numbers of people.

Follower numbers are nothing, thirst is everything. First quench people's thirst.

Placing ads on Twitter? No, thanks. I think Twitter has a bigger mission completely directed at the individual in terms of marketing communications.

First we need to sort that out.

SOCIAL VIDEO SHARING PLATFORMS

Youtube

After the blog which is our main base, Facebook which receive all kinds of communication materials with open arms and Twitter on which we exist with our short texts, now is the time for our unique social medium Youtube which serves us with visual and auditory materials.

Yes, words are important. Yes, one image is worth a thousand words. Yet, nothing beats the taste of the combination of audio and moving image. Some of us like to read but all of us love to watch video in general. You can convey a message that you would have to give in a long text with a video in a much shorter time and while doing so, you can touch much more points of the human brain.

When the subject is social media the first video platform that comes to mind is Youtube. Although it has many look-a-likes, Youtube is the most traffic receiving website compared to the other video portals due to being the first and its compatibility with Google as well as its infrastructure. That is why if there is video involved in the job, brands need to use Youtube actively as well. Well, how should you use Youtube in your social media strategies?

In general, there is a mantra on everyone's lips about shooting viral videos. Brands are also pretty convinced of the urban legend that goes around saying "shooting viral video is a very simple job and moreover it is free." There are lots of people around saying "We should shoot a viral video and put it on Youtube, then wait for the millions to watch it!" Everybody who has a brilliant idea thinks that this could be transformed into a viral video.

But the truth of the matter is different. Viral videos are not that easy to create as you might be assuming. Turn a deaf ear to the urban legends going around. If you shoot a video such as "Oglum bak git" you can create a viral effect and get a million hits. But I don't know if you would consider shooting a video like this if you are manufacturing vacuum cleaners. There surely must be a relation between your brand image and the vacuum cleaner which is being smashed on somebody's head.

Unfortunately, many simple ideas that could turn into a viral video loose their taste and meaning after they have been evaluated by the management of the firms. The ones which don't loose their taste, on the other hand, loose their budget balance at the end. After tens of meetings, you suddenly see that budgets have swollen up. When budget swell up, the viral video concept starts to loose the meaning it has for the management. From the perspective of the management, this means spending money from their pockets. Beautiful ideas become nothing at the end and get lost in the infinite sea of ideas before they are actualized.

The truth is that, there is no such thing as viral video being cheap and without a budget. Oldspice shot a 33 second TV ad and got over forty millions of hits by putting it on Youtube.

Similarly, Volkswagen's production with Darth Vader had more than fifty million displays up to the minute. Fifty millions is easier said than done. Are these cheap productions? We'll see.

Is there anyone here who hasn't watched the cute Panda who turns the lives of people who don't buy its product to hell? Just search for "Never Say No to Panda" on Youtube.

Do you know what the best part of this is? These videos may have already been broadcasted on TV and left the screen but people still continue to watch these fun videos on the Internet.

Let's get back to the matter of cheapness. All three productions are well-thought, well-designed and have substantial budgets. Well, are they viral? Yes they are viral. They are funny, sincere, elaborate and surprising. We all like to watch such videos and want our friends to watch them as well. That is why we share this kind of videos on our social accounts such as Facebook and Twitter.

Result: Viral video doesn't mean video which has been shot in an amateur way with a hand camera. Productions with budgets may also be viral. You don't shoot viral video. You shoot a video and then it becomes viral. Well-thought, elaborate productions with high quality as well as powerful subject and expression will always give good results. Besides viral is a matter of strategy. If there is a viral design in a marketing plan, there isn't a necessity for it to be a video too. However, no matter what is planned as viral, it should be designed thoroughly and correctly from the beginning to the end and beyond.

Get used to produce videos

Let's come to the subject we will discuss about Youtube by finishing viral video chit chat here. Our subject is producing videos again, but this time more pragmatic and different. What we will do is very simple; to tell the job we are doing with video.

Let's suppose that you are not able to produce viral video due to the obstructive factors we've listed above; then you should better tell what you are doing by using video. Whatever your passion, your field of expertise is, just talk about it in front of a camera. Are you one of the people who cannot talk to the camera? Then listen to what I'm going to tell you.

P-Arch is a client of mine I offer consultancy services about digital marketing communications which designs hotels and stores and implements what is designed on the site. They have Caffe Nero, Starbucks and many other important chain clients in their portfolio. P-Arch hasn't had a marketing implementation other than sectoral magazines until we met. They were not so much aware of the benefit they could get from social media during our first meeting. What they did was quite ordinary for them since they were all experts in their jobs. It was me who first felt that they were doing an extraordinary job as I was far removed from the architecture sector. I told them they that they were actually working in a field that would sound different to the people from outside and that would arouse interest. They told me in response that they did not have an effective area to market since they were not working for the final consumer. They have already lost their excitement about marketing their work due to the professional blindness that could happen to all of us who are in the center. Moreover, what kind of a story they had to tell anyway?

During the later hours of our first meeting they told me about their job as if it was as normal as making tea; how they constructed cafés, their design processes, how they ordered furniture to be made rapidly, how they made the cafés ready for service in ten day by working day and night, how the team worked with all their might and how all the operations went on without any interruption. It is exciting, isn't it? (If you are an architect, I wouldn't know of course.) When I proposed to make a video out of this whole process, they were surprised at first and then asked me: "Why?"

The reason was pretty simple for me: this was their passion and no matter how ordinary it was for them, it was very extraordinary and interesting for someone looking from outside. Additionally, this potential would catch potential customer's attention too.

We didn't have the power to shoot a superb video. Under these circumstances, I asked them to take photos whenever they started a new construction and send me the photos together with a short text about the job to be done there. Similarly, I asked them to take photos of the completed work as well. In this way, we would have "Before" and "After" images to use. Now, it was only a matter of transforming these photos to video. And we've solved this problem with Movie Maker which comes as a standard with Windows. After putting the photos on the program and adding a background music, the work was completed. We spent 20 minutes to make the video. We spent just as much to upload it on Youtube. At the end, we had a video of one minute and twelve seconds. When it was time to give a title to video, we used credits and a clear description as I always prefer to use (in a way people would think to search on search engines). (The name of the work, the name of the firm which is doing the work; JeansLab Espark Eskisehir Branch, P-Arch Architecture.)

You can think that the name wouldn't be that much important. You would be surprized to see the results when you write "JeansLab Espark" on Google. Still, when only "JeansLab Espark" is searched, P-Arch welcomes people on the third row with its Youtube video with its substantial content.

"Welcome" says P-Arch to the ones searching "JeansLab Espark" on Google. "We are the firm who made inner decoration of this place!"

THE KEY POINT: TO PRODUCE CONTENT

What I want to say based on this example is that you don't need to make a big production or go in front of the camera in order to make a video. Believe me that there is tens of video works you can produce as above until you reach that point. I repeat: If you intend to make a video production, there is no obligation for it to be viral. Think simple. Bring the photos together. And just like that, your video would be ready.

Youtube is the most popular video portal today. It lost some of its viewers in Turkey when it was banned but Youtube is still our main drag when it comes to video. Google shows videos related to the word you search on the first page, if there is any.

You must have understood by now that the job always comes back to produce content and Google closes the deal at the end of the day.

People would want to watch the videos first if they encounter videos related to their interests or the subject they are making searches about. Watching videos is easier than reading texts. People like to watch videos. Some of your videos would be watched a hundred times, some a thousand, and some twenty thousand times just as the video named "The critique of the movie, Conquest 1453"[25] we shot as 3 buddies ... All videos have audiences, more or less. Audience means potential customer.

Just try to make videos about your job, hobby or brand. There will always be people who want to watch what you offer. How to videos, what is videos, promotional videos, recommendation videos, funny videos, suggestion videos... All this would work. If you cannot do anything, just collect photos and make a video out of those as I mentioned above. Go after your passion. Here is another successful example for you: A domestic e-commerce website which makes digital prints on canvas, Canvastar [26]brought together the works of famous painters in a similar way and uploaded it on Youtube. Canvastar's Youtube channel's rating was over two hundred thousand as I was writing these sentences and they mostly sell abroad right now. Wonder why?

Today, it is very enjoyable for me to see that P-Arch

added new clients on its portfolio thanks to these videos and continues to gain new ones everyday. Moreover, their videos are not viral. This is something that could happen to all the corporations who made a similar effort. The only thing you need is a simple video processing software. And Windows Movie Maker is not the only solution for that. There are tens of programs on Internet which enable you to process video. Youtube's own video editor comes first. Try if you have the desire.

OTHER VIDEO SITES

I've gathered tens of video sharing sites under one title: Other Video Sites. Would you complain about this? Actually, I am making your work easier. Otherwise, we would be unable to work all this out. Usually, the biggest error firms and agencies make is to try to be on all of these sites... There is no need for you to be on Youtube, Vimeo or Dailymotion all at once with a video you've shot. Of course you would want to be on more similar media once you enter to this world and - I'll talk about this later - there is no end to this. Additionally, you shouldn't forget that you would loose perception and focus if you distribute yourself on all media. I call this video spamming.

My recommendation would be for you to share your videos on one foreign and one domestic video sharing site. That way, your address would be known and you wouldn't distract people's focus. Moreover, you would be saving energy.

In the past years, we've produced a video and uploaded it on all the video sites we know to test their ratings. After we shot and uploaded the video on the sites, we didn't even look back to the video for months. Months later, we analyzed the ratings of the videos we've done nothing to promote.

Here are the results: It is enough for you to upload your videos on Youtube globally and on one video site locally.

I repeat: for your video content sharing strategies, it is enough for you to upload your videos on one foreign and one domestic social video sharing site. If you insist on trying different sites, I would recommend Viddler. Viddler is a more customizable video platform. It is different than the classical ones. On Viddler, you are able to tag certain minutes of your video with key words for example. In this way, you are doing a favor for the ones who want to watch certain parts of the video by tagging important moments in the changing scenario of the video. Let's suppose you are going to talk about different subjects in a single video and your video is pretty long. In this case, you can tag the starting moment of each subject separately. If you are interested in the second subject in the video, you can click on that part directly and start to watch from there on. And comments could be tagged on certain moments of the video by the audience as well on Viddler. In other words, you are able to leave your comment on the moment/second of the video that you want to comment on and not on the whole of it.

Facebook, Twitter and Youtube. Are you getting confused? There are other social platforms I will be talking about in the next pages. We will discuss the correct usage of social media as well on the oncoming chapters of the book. Which medium should be used in what way, where should we be? Are all the media suitable for every corporation or brand? We shouldn't get confused as media multiply.

We proceed with live streaming over the Internet.

LIVE STREAMING OVER INTERNET: USTREAM.TV

Yes, you've heard it right: live streaming. Now, you don't need to spend so much effort with hundreds of PR agencies in order to talk about your product for five minutes by participating live broadcasts on TVs. You can make your own live broadcast yourself. The only thing you need for this is a little computer camera and Ustream.

You can go to Ustream.tv now and create your own channel. (Youtube started to give the same service too.) If you have a certain program format on your mind, you can gather your audience in front of the screen at the time you will start broadcasting by announcing this on your blog or on other social media platforms. Moreover, you can get questions and messages during the live broadcast in this way; you can progress according to the answers you will give to these questions. The ones who missed the program shouldn't be upset about this as well. For, you will be able to record your live broadcast by just one press of a button for reruns. In this way, nobody will miss the program and you will have a nice archive for yourself.

Are you a real estate agent? Just sit and talk about the real estate market in your region with your team mates. Don't forget to present your portfolio by the way. Are you a tourism agency? Talk about what kind of holidays you have on your portfolio, what you offer or your campaigns during the seasons. Tell stories about the places you've been. Chat about where to go in which country.

If you would make an announcement such as "I will be presenting top 10 holiday destinations for families with children in Antalya for the summer season just in a moment on live broadcast" on your Facebook page and Twitter account, I bet there will be tens of people who would watch your show.

There is no reason for our silly program "Kirmizi Koltuk - The Red Sofa", -which was a program we've started to produce just for fun in order to critique the feature movies- not to turn into a live broadcast after the attention it attracted on Youtube.

Well but will we have any audience? We cannot know for sure without trying. Why wouldn't it be watched on live broadcast if it is being watched on Youtube? There are people who are making money by producing programs on Ustream.tv right now.

Just think about it; you are a real estate agent and you make such an announcement on your Facebook page and Twitter: "We will give very special information about decreasing real estate prices in Clifton on live broadcast at 16:30! The cheapest apartments... Coming up next!"

I swear I would be watching as a person who is trying to purchase a house even if nobody watches. I would try to watch it later, as soon as I can even if I miss it. Even the next day could be too late to watch (if I have money in my pocket of course.) For, the question on my mind would be: What if people who watch it before me go and buy those apartments before me?

SOCIAL PRESENTATION SHARING PLATFORMS

Slideshare and Slideboom

If producing a video is too hard for you, you should at least prepare a presentation. Are you able to prepare Powerpoint or Keynote presentations? OK then. Unfortunately, social presentation sharing sites do not take much place in social media plans of social media agencies and firms today. Yet, I must say that these are very important platforms strategically. There are tens of websites with similar functions but the prominent ones are Slideshare and Slideboom.

Both of them are websites which allow you to upload your presentations in formats such as Powerpoint, pdf etc.

You enable everybody to watch your presentations by doing this. In other words, you are socializing your presentations.

For example, I constantly share my training notes, seminar and conference presentations on Slideshare. I am followed by like-minded individuals or interested students in my field of expertise just as it is in other social media, I get comments, I interact with them and maybe I get more conference invites by doing so.

Of course, it is possible to adapt this platform to the usage of brands. You can prepare presentations in the field you are passionate about in a similar way to video production and draw attention of those who want to find you in this way.

If a tourist guide would prepare an English presentation titled "10 historical sites to see in Istanbul", this would attract the attention of hundreds, maybe even thousands of tourists who plan to come to Istanbul. To have made this presentation would make our guide one of the first guides to be preferred as an expert in the field.

For a furniture manufacturer, a presentation titled "The Trendiest Corner Sets of 2012" would draw the attention of the ones who want to buy new furniture for their living rooms. Or, if you are selling aquarium fish, prepare a presentation titled "Fish species which could live in the same aquarium" and upload this on Slideshare or Slideboom. Believe me that many people who are interested in aquariums would click on this presentation and many of them would contact you.

There is an iPhone & iPad application named "Text Here",[27] which you can use both for work and fun by adding speech bubbles on photos and images and easily marking them. This app has a very fun area of usage in the daily lives of people. Yet, people have a very limited understanding of it as if the application consists of only the text found on iTunes page and the images that belong to it unless you explain it to them. If a presentation titled "The Areas of Usage of the iOS App Text Here" was to be prepared and this presentation was to be supported by exemplary images prepared by Text Here, I can guarantee that many people would be interested in it and download the app just due to the curiosity aroused with this presentation. These examples may be multiplied. Just, don't forget to add a link at the end of your presentations or videos to your blog or website, whichever is your main base.

Google link values of the presentation sites are also very high. People love to watch "How to do?" style presentations. You will be surprised to the traffic that will be coming to your website from the presentations you put on Slideshare and Slideboom.

Do you own a publishing house? Try to put the presentations of the books you have on your portfolio on Slideshare and Slideboom.

You can prepare as much presentation as you want in your field of expertise and upload on these sites. It is enough for you to have passion about that field. It wouldn't be bad at all if I prepared a presentation titled "The Most Genuine Eating Places of the Last Three Years" for Harbiyiyorum, would it?

SOCIAL IMAGE SHARING PLATFORMS

Flickr

Flickr, which was acquired by Yahoo from Ludicorp in 2005 for $35 million and which made Yahoo proud, is an image sharing site with the most photos on it according to the data of 2010 with a figure over five billion. Despite its acting against the spirit of social media and losing my sympathy by giving limited sharing space to its free members and limitless sharing space to its paid members, Flickr is still one of the most popular visual social media sharing platforms. The reason of its popularity is its being the first in this field and bloggers' use of this site as a photo archive for years. It is another example to show the fact that the first in the market always wins... Flickr's strongest suit is still its content although it is being pulled down with each passing day by other visual social media sharing sites which provide more features. This content continues to provide a traffic enabling it to stay on Alexa 100. That is why you would still benefit even if you upload your photos only on this site and give links to your website from here.

Flickr is essentially a photo sharing platform. Video sharing was also allowed on the site as of 2008. Yet, I absolutely wouldn't recommend this. It is really unfortunate for Flickr to have made this decision. Don't forget that we already have separate video sharing sites for videos. Flickr is only for social image sharing. Let's not get sidetracked.

Yes, we've uploaded our images on Flickr. Later, we can enter descriptions under each image we've uploaded and increase our website's traffic by giving links to our main base (blog, website). Moreover, if we are to publish our photos by enabling everybody to see them, we will be accessible for millions of people who make searches on Flickr and have similar interests. These people would want to contact us by clicking on our blog link written on the description field of the image after viewing the photos. Moreover, we are able to arouse interest about ourselves by commenting on other people's photos in our field of interest. This approach would bring us new people who want to contact us about our products and services.

Architecture, fine arts, jewelry, ornament, accessories, design, food, photography, etc. No matter which visually attractive job you are involved in, Flickr and similar platforms constitute important social marketing channels for you.

Picasa

Google's service Picasa is of course more advantageous in terms of its offerings compared to Flickr. There is a world of difference between

Flickr has 1 Terabyte image storing capacity and Google has 15 gigabytes of image storing capacity. These two can make you fly.

You can use Picasa to archive your photos in albums just as you can in Flickr. If you upload your images by enabling everybody to see them, you would be enabling opportunities to create interactions related to your products and services just as I said under the Flickr title. However, don't forget to mark "Everybody" on the part where you are asked to choose who should see your photos in your privacy settings while you are uploading them.

You can view images tagged under various category titles and leave comments for them on Picasa. I suppose there is no need for me to repeat that you should direct people to your main base on which you are making your sales with the descriptions you write for the photos.

Besides, you have the opportunity to download and use Picasa on your computer as desktop software enabling visual editing. You can also share the photos you've edited on Google+ which is considered as the Facebook of Google with only one press of a button.

Google makes itself felt with the services it offers alongside with its search engine feature. Although Picasa is seen to be coming as second after Flickr since Flickr was the first visual sharing platform in the field, the number of users of Picasa is too high to be underestimated.

Just try. And use whichever you like.

Pinterest

There was not even the "P" of Pinterest as I started writing this book. When Pinterest started to shine in the early days of 2012, I was giving seminars on "the correct usage of social media". Of course Pinterest wasn't being mentioned in these seminars.

As a person who follows trends and new ventures, I constantly try to introduce the things I like on SMN (SosyalMedyaNedir.net). I had discovered Pinterest when I was doing a research for SMN and registered as a member in September 2011.

When digital and conventional media started to talk about Pinterest as a rising new medium and how it is the strongest social medium after Facebook and Twitter, I looked back and saw that I had an account on it even though I did nothing with it. Honestly, I thought that Pinterest is no great shakes in terms of social media at the beginning. Additionally, we used to have conversations with friends who are also experts in this field about the bright futures of tens of other social media ventures. Yet, Pinterest's name wasn't mentioned within these promising social media platforms.

However, I can say that I learned a great lesson from exactly this point on the sudden rising of Pinterest. No matter how much we follow the trends or how many futurists we have around us, nobody has an idea about what a certain medium's future will be next year. This could of course be generalized for the future of every other thing as well. Today, Pinterest is considered as the third strongest medium after Facebook and Twitter. This seems to me partly as sector's pumping. Of course the rising of a third powerful player in the market after Facebook and Twitter is a pretty motivating development for all kinds of new ventures and the investors of these. As you know, everybody has a "start-up" dream nowadays. Everybody who has an original idea and project dreams of being a millionaire in two years after receiving funding from some angel investor. This is why we can say that Pinterest has been a nice rev up for all the entrepreneurs and the angel investors.

I prepared a presentation titled "Social Media and Blindness to Change" on which I worked for a long time since I wasn't able to see the rise of Pinterest and started talking about it in seminars. You can probably guess its content. It was about people's inability to see the rise of "Pinterest" among all these social media platforms, moreover about how people were unable to see important changes within the abundance of the flow of information. Human brain was focusing on one or two social media sites of importance in order to be able to protect itself among hundreds of social media increasing in number every passing day. Therefore, my one and only recommendation to the audience during these presentations was that they shouldn't exhaust themselves to much in order to learn and try everything. Big players are already being brought to you by the sector. Even if you think you see shining stars within all the others from far away, the main media are always being put in front of you by the sector like the sun. Don't push yourselves to much!

Right now, Pinterest ranks higher than Flickr among visual sharing sites according to the data of Alexa. In other words, it can be considered as a very important medium for brands' marketing activities.

Pinterest's difference from other visual sharing sites is its style of presenting images. Just think of having a pin board of a limitless size. Every picture you pin on your board pushes down the pictures you've added before. There are millions of people who follow and pin the images they are interested in on Pinterest just like Facebook and Twitter. If others like the images you've pinned on your board, they can re-pin them on their own boards. So, we are able to create a viral pyramid scheme just as on every successful social media platforms.

The people who sell fast moving consumer goods, designers, artists, e-commerce websites and group shopping sites have begun to take their places rapidly on Pinterest. If you are one of them, you should better check out Pinterest.

While using Pinterest for your brand
Along with Pinterest came the trend of brands creating visual expressions of the matters related to their own field of expertise. These are called Infographic-Information Graphics. Probably, infographics were not as popular as they are now before Pinterest. Infographics are very effective promotional tools today in terms of content. The information you provide with a graphic expression in your field of expertise continues to be shared in an endless cycle on pin boards of people who are interested in that subject on Pinterest.

You are able to access millions of images on basis of category at the moment you enter to Pinterest. You are able to see the images shared by your friends. You are able to share the ones you like on your board. In short, you collect images on your board as if you are actually gathering a collection together. And there is an interesting piece of information spreading like wildfire. It is being said that 80% of Pinterest users are women. In other words, Pinterest is a market for women. This makes Pinterest a unique blessing for the e-commerce websites which are especially selling products to women for showcasing their portfolios and drawing attention of their potential and existing clients. It has already been included in social media communication plans of the companies especially in vertical markets (product oriented firms).

For example, do you sell jewellery; or do you sell oil

painting, antiques, shoes or watches? If I were you, I wouldn't miss a beat and I would start to move my entire portfolio to Pinterest right away. If I was selling cosmetic products, I would put the photos of the models I've implemented various make-up examples on with my own products. Pinterest has the structure to direct people rapidly to sales if you manage to feed it with your new creations and new products.

Above all, Pinterest is a very powerful backlink provider for your main base (your website or blog). Aside from all this, you are able to pin not only images but videos on your board as well on Pinterest. Everything you like including video clips, promotional videos etc. You can either upload the image or video you want to share from your computer, or you can copy-paste the link of the image or video on the related field and that is all you have to do in order to "pin" that content.

Content, Sincerity and the First Step

If you ask me how I use Pinterest as a marketing professional, I would say that I share the photos of food I am using on Harbiyiyorum.com for example. The photos of food I shot draw the attention of some food-lovers and this attracts new visitors to my website. In addition, I write comments under the food photos shared by others. Or I pin the ones I like on my own board. In this way, I gain their interest in my own shares. Moreover, we prepare infographics related to iPhone apps we develop as a corporation. To share these on Pinterest is in the nature of the business. To give an example, we published an infographic titled "How to Prepare an Effective CV?" when we've released iOS app named "Prepare CV".

If I were a designer, I would share all the work I've shared on my blog on Pinterest as well and I would gain more traffic to my main base by doing so. Are you making sales over E-bay or Etsy? Don't waist time. Just pin all your products on Pinterest.

Misapplications on Pinterest

Based on the experiences from Facebook and Twitter, I come to the conclusion that the brands don't understand the nature of this media clearly. Their actions on Pinterest point to this fact as well. This is actually normal since as the number of social media increases, people get confused as I've been telling in "Blindness to Change".

It is not correct for the brands to conduct campaigns to increase their follower numbers on Pinterest as they do on Facebook and Twitter. This is only a waist of time. Instead of conducting campaigns on Pinterest as you do on Facebook, conduct Twitter Searches, develop Facebook applications, think of good content to produce videos for Youtube. You are not obliged to conduct activities to increase the number of your followers on Pinterest because it has become popular just as you do on Facebook pages. There is no such a rule that says every social media site will function in the same way.

Pinterest is not to be used in that way. Moreover, you won't be able to use something you don't spend much time with. Each and every social medium has different grounds and triggers different spots on our brains. One needs to understand the spirit of each.

Instagram

As mobile use increases every day, we have encountered a social image sharing network only usable by smart phone owners: Instagram. Yes, unfortunately you cannot use Instagram over the web.

Established in the last quarter of 2010, Instagram has been released as a very user-friendly mobile phone app which brought the Polaroid of old days together with digital effects. Thanks to this app, even people who have no talent for taking photos are able to capture great frames. You can rapidly share your photos on leading social networks as well as easily adding effects to your photos on Instagram. While smart phones' camera technologies constantly improve together with the devices, aesthetic perception has begun to increase immensely thanks to Instagram's digital filters. I can even say that we've jumped at least ten years ahead.

The firm which was established at the last quarter of 2010 first developed the app only for iPhone and iPad as a free of charge add-in.

Right after the announcement of the launch of Android version in the April of 2012, it was acquired by Facebook for $1 billion (or vice versa.) It is great, isn't it? Less than two years later of its establishment, it is being acquired by a giant such as Facebook.

Facebook had to make that move since it was aware of the fact that the future was in the mobile industry. The ones using Google Analytics would know. Today, you see a section named "Mobile" when you enter to your websites to view the statistics of your visitors. You can see the data concerning the smart phones on which you had visits to your website. If you monitor this data, you will see how the visitors using mobile phones increase in numbers with your own eyes.

As a person who was selling paintings before, what I like the most about Instagram is its editing in frame format and therefore providing a continuous standardization in images. The standardization of such a customizable content in terms of dimensions means that new business areas will be born out of this. We are already witnessing the examples of these. This standardization is like the magic touch of Jesus for printed customizable souvenir sector such as posters, paintings, magnets etc.

For example, you are able to order your photos on Instagram as canvas prints thanks to InstaCanvas. Or you are able to transform your Instagram photos into fridge magnets thanks to Stickygram. I immediately ordered a magnet series from my favorite Instagram photos at the sight of this service. Don't be surprised if you see standard Instagram frames in big shopping malls and framers soon. We are all artists now thanks to smart phones. It is very natural for us to want to see the photos we've taken on the walls of our houses. The trend is increasingly going towards customizable products in the field of souvenirs. And platforms such as Instagram provide the standardization needed for these additional services.

You can use Instagram in terms of marketing similarly to Pinterest by writing comments on people's photos, by following them and by putting photos of your own products. And if you enter tags (#hashtags) under the photos as comments, you will see that more people are interested in your photos and that your interaction increases on this platform. Additionally, Instagram determines certain themes through #hashtags especially on weekends, motivates people to take photos on that theme, and later publishes these photos on its own blog.

Just search for #graduation hashtag on Instagram to view some of the graduation ceremonies all over the world.

Brand campaigns on Instagram

Similarly, brands may also conduct their own photo campaigns on Instagram using this tagging logic. Believe me you will see better results than the most creative and most liked shots you see in photo contests organized on Facebook. Pepsi-Co has already conducted a work with #briskpic hashtag for its newly introduced Icetea. Similarly, Redbull conducted a campaign with its #redbullwinter hashtag. You can also make your own crowd on your existing social networks use the advantages of this application and experience a superior image sharing process both from the perspective of the brand and of the users.

You have probably noticed how effective it was for my blog's promotion my tagging my own food photos with the words #food and #kebab based on the primitive state of these campaign ideas.

There isn't a standard way to enter to Instagram as a brand. However don't waist time; take the photos of your own products and seek fun ways to present them. The smart phones in your hands are miraculous tools just as Moses' staff which parted the Red Sea. You are able to produce original and creative content suitable for every medium continuously with the apps developed for these phones. For example, you can make inanimate objects talk using speech bubbles of Text Here iOS app and create your own cartoons in order to facilitate the marketing of your products.

Yes, now you have made your products speak through photos and transformed them by filters and effects to attract the attention of more people. The only thing left to do is to post them on all the social image sharing platforms. This is also a good way to exist on social networks. You don't need to organize campaigns necessarily. For example, Levi's Brazil and Starbucks are using Instagram by putting the photos they shot according to their own brand communication tones.

Levi's publishes photos of people with a style wearing Levi's and walking down the street. They don't even hesitate to tag some of the photos with #assoftheday hashtag. Brands, please be brave and don't hesitate to share your photos. And don't be afraid of the comments you will get from people too. As the saying goes: Cowards die many times before their deaths!

Today, Instagram gave some of the features of Photoshop to our hands for free. Don't forget; you will get ten times of the effect a normal photo can get thanks to this app.

Linkedin: The big shot of social media

Of course there were other business networks before Linkedin made its appearance on the arena. Yet, none of them succeeded in shining as bright as Linkedin. Linkedin stood out amongst other professional business networks and came to the fore together with rising social media.

Linkedin as the big shot of social media is a social business network on which the people with the most successful careers in the world are at the forefront with their professional business lives. You complete the pyramid scheme with your first degree contacts, second and third degree connections on Linkedin.

The only thing I can say about Linkedin is that it is a platform which gives you the opportunity to prepare a CV compatible with social media and shows the big shot in you on the contrary to your profiles on Facebook and Twitter. Yet, Linkedin can never replace Facebook or Twitter. The reason is quite simple: it is not fun!

You cannot share your kids' photos, post music videos or send funny videos about sports on Linkedin. A formal atmosphere prevails there.

If you are a corporation, it would be wiser to use Linkedin from the perspective of Human Resources. You can easily see references of the individuals and their connections till sixth degree. It would be enough for you to create a corporate page here and share formal things such as corporate video, address, announcement, notice etc. by consulting your Human Resources department.

As an individual, it would be better if you synchronize your personal Facebook and Twitter accounts with Linkedin after you create your CV. Linkedin is a place where people talk about business and do so in a formal tone. That is why you should conduct your offers, projects, business on Linkedin rather than Facebook and Twitter. In other words, professional matters will be taken more seriously here compared to Facebook and Twitter. If you don't have a first degree connection with someone on Linkedin, you won't be able to send a message to them, so you either have to request from someone you have a first degree connection to introduce you to them or upgrade your account by paying a monthly fee to Linkedin. Money solves every problem as you know. Similarly, the one who pays in Linkedin is able to own the whole pyramid scheme. Additionally, Linkedin guarantees that you will get an answer from the people you send messages to if you upgrade your membership to a paid one. (I haven't tried that and I am not sure how realistic this promise of Linkedin is. May I ask the people who have tried it to contact me from @Temurah?)

Moreover, there are lots of groups created on the basis of the fields of expertise on Linkedin. You can become a member to these groups according to your own industry. You can follow supply, demand and chat and make your offers whenever you deem it necessary or participate in meetings. You would be expanding your professional circle in this way.

You can see job openings on Facebook or Twitter and even, review of your Facebook and Twitter account could be enough for the position you are interested in. Yet, some corporations could prefer to consider the information you have on Linkedin primarily. The most important point here is to understand the grounds of the related tools and to know where each of these would work the best. Remember, you are going to play the role of a big shot on Linkedin.

Everybody has a big shot in them. Just support the big shot in you using Linkedin.

Linkedin ads

When it comes to the Linkedin ads, I can say that the

process functions more or less in a similar way to the process in Facebook. You define your credit card and create your ad step by step. The only difference is that Linkedin does not support ads in multi-languages at the moment. In other words, you have to place ads in English even if you are going to sell something with a Greek content. In this case, giving ads for abroad seems more appropriate. Just do it if you are not bothered with your ad text being in English. (We are expecting a move from Linkedin on this matter) - While this book was being prepared for printing, we heard the news about Linkedin ads now being published in different languages.

In addition, you are able to narrow down the audience of your ad on Linkedin on the basis of firm, country, gender, field of profession and group membership. In this way, you can use your ad with a more effective performance. You don't have the opportunity on Linkedin such as giving the ad for a certain area as Facebook pages or for the content you share on the page. In other words, you necessarily have to direct your ad to a website or Landing Page.

Linkedin ads are accessible through "Advertising" part that can be found at the bottom of the page. There are many expert agencies providing ad infrastructure with Turkish content for Linkedin as there is for various social media. Getting support from these firms will save you time. Additionally, you will be using your budget in a more effective way thanks to optimized ads.

LOCATION BASED SERVICES

We started to see programs just like the ones on our desktops thanks to the platforms developed for various phone brands together with the increasing popularity of smart phones. However, the name for the ones on desktop is

"Programs" while this word was replaced with "Applications" on mobile phones. While desktop computers are transforming into palmtop computers, firms started to develop special apps for these palmtop computers.

And after GPS (Global Positioning System) technology was added on top of all these developments, the story began to flow in a totally different direction. This technology which was first developed by scientists with the purpose of determining the locations of the satellites reached the position it has today with the question of "Why don't we do the exact opposite of this? Won't it be great if the satellites find us?" And nothing was ever the same after that. Now, every individual with a smart phone was able to tell the satellite their exact location with a deviation of one meter (of course as long as they had their phones with them.)

As this was the case and smart phones started to play an increasingly big role in our lives, we started to see applications with a little sprinkle of social media on them. Today, Foursquare comes first to our minds when the subject is "location based services" in social media. Let's see what made Foursquare so popular.

Foursquare

Foursquare, which was founded in 2009 with the thought of taking advantage of the mobile devices and GPS technology to enable people's interaction with their environment, is actually the real-time, evolved model of the famous Monopoly on mobile phones.

It is an application in which you collect points by "Checking in" places you have around you and inform people about your whereabouts by saying "I'm here!", and you can even become the "Mayor" of a place by collecting certain amount of check-ins. You get a certain virtual honor in the places you've become mayor on Foursquare as well. So, doesn't it really sound like Monopoly? Moreover, you are able to win many virtual badges by fulfilling other criteria like this. For example, if you make a "Check-in" with your friends at the same time, you get extra points and you also win a "badge" related to your status.

Although I don't care much about getting points and winning badges, I have once more understood that the new generation has a very different perspective on these matters after I heard a student of mine saying "I really like getting points on Foursquare. I also care about being mayor of a place as much as I care about points." Not only that, I've heard such talks many times from others as well after this conversation. In short, people love check-ins of Foursquare. They feel as happy as kids who got their school reports at the end of the year when they win virtual badges. Today, millions of people see where their friends have been and done during the day and satisfy their curiosity while also winning gifts through virtual reflections of their real lives.

Millions of people use this application right now. It is pretty popular in Turkey as well. Foursquare shines brightly as a real-time service based on the relationship between the individual and the environment with the help of GPS. This naturally attracts the attention of marketing professionals in terms of momentary movements in places. At the end, they have a lot to gain from this.

For example, you are able to leave "Tips" (comments) for the places you've been on Foursquare. In this way, anybody who goes to a place you have left a comment for and checks-in, are able to read your comment about that place. Although most of the places with comments seem as complaint and wailing walls, there is always a chance of encountering right-minded comments you would enjoy reading. There are some very funny tips as well. For example, I enjoy the tip you would see if you check-in to Kanyon Starbucks that says "Their toast with double Mihalic (A special Turkish cheese that is not available in any Starbucks at all) cheese is very good. Push them for it! Note: Search them under the counter." The smartly written tips with humor enter to the popular tip category in time. Remember that Foursquare is a fun place. The things you write about your complaints and dissatisfactions won't be much popular there.

The effect Foursquare has is to create a virtual value with regard to the place you are at. The most correct thing to do is to act with this thought in mind while using the application. The strongest weapon of marketing professionals while creating this value would be to leave masterful tips at the places related to your sector as I mentioned before in previous chapters. Of course, if you have a restaurant or a coffee shop, it would be effective to organize campaigns such as "One ultra deluxe coffee is free of charge for the ones who check-in with their friends!" but the real deadly marketing effect would be created by asking to food & beverage places nearby whether they have tried the ultra deluxe coffee of the brand X or not and leaving a comment on the related places. Still, I would recommend you to avoid leaving standard comments everywhere. Read what has been said about the place first and then leave a comment specific to that place by looking at the tones of people who have talked about that place. Otherwise, you would be spamming. Leave smartly written comments. Just like the ones you enjoy when you read.

Of course, the comments I leave at certain places as Harbiyiyorum draws attention of the people who go to these places and read the tips. For example, I lead people to Harbiyiyorum in order for them to discover more places like the place I left a comment for right after I write the comment. Sometimes, it is even enough to say "Harbiyiyorum was here" under the places I've been and ate.

If I was responsible for the marketing of a frozen food production firm, I would create a team on site and send them to all the restaurants that use our products, and then make them write on Foursquare under those places: "This restaurant uses XXX brand's products. Have peace of mind while eating and enjoy." Or if I was a domestic furniture manufacturer, I would go to IKEA on Foursquare and write "Enjoy your new wardrobe. Now you are going to go home and spend your time trying to install it-XXX Furniture." Or if I had an energy drink brand, I would write under all the entertainment places and sport complexes like this: "Hey, have fun guys! Youth means energy and power. Just remember that XXX is always there for you whenever you feel your energy is running out."

By the way, I would like to mention one more thing. The tips you leave on Foursquare are being published without passing through the approval of an editor.

The ones who've read Seth Godin's Purple Cow would know. In this book, Seth is especially talking about the dullness of the marketing sector he is in and the need for a change in this area. The book offers us methods to get rid of the conventional and boring marketing approach. Its general discourse revolves around creating differences in marketing but the book is more like the prayer of a marketing professional who got sick and tired of the silliness that goes on around him.

Today, 10 years later Seth Godin's book, I see that social media has managed to rescue marketing from this monotony. In other words, Seth Godin's mantras have been accepted. When the famous marketer wrote this book, social media was only in the stage of incubation and actually what Seth was looking for was exactly this excitement social media creates today for marketing professionals. All social media tools offer you the opportunity to create instantaneous excitement and to reach masses on the contrary of conventional media which have taken over the corners. Foursquare is included to these.

You might say: what if the competitors do the same? I am talking about leaving comments on places on Foursquare.

You should have noticed by now that all the subjects we've talked about till now are challenging and demanding things to do.

All the work you'll be doing on Foursquare will be as demanding as others and the coast is still clear. Whoever acts now would grab the leadership. Moreover, this is not an easy thing to do. And above all, it is not something you can request from social media agencies easily or demand the results right away. It requires planned work, constituting a team, concentration, intense labor and later, following-up. The content of your comments is also very important. You can upset the apple-cart at a single stroke.

After all, we don't see many people succeeding since the "labor" part is always being underestimated in spite of the fact that all the things I've mentioned are exciting things. As I've mentioned earlier, the marketing executives of corporations are not able to think long-reaching probably due to pressures that are created on them related to numbers. All social media definitely require a long-term strategy and a planned work.

And Foursquare is definitely very suitable to the spirit of this job (leaving comments). I wouldn't want you to interpret what I am saying here as if I don't attach importance to the campaigns conducted on Foursquare. Of course you can award your customers who make check-ins by organizing campaigns and work to increase your sales but the job of writing comment is something that could be implemented on almost every sector and for every brand. If you are a firm which manufactures chimneys, for example, awarding a prize to the ones who make check-ins wouldn't mean much for your business probably.

Greenpeace supported its campaign titled "How big is yours?" which aimed at preventing the hunt of undersized fishes on Foursquare by writing informative comments regarding the subject matter on the frequently visited places such as Istiklal Street [28] and fish restaurants. This made the job very effective both on conventional media and on social media. This work is one of the best examples of the correct usage of social media and Foursquare. We all took our hats off to them.

Mekanist (The clone of Yelp.com)

There is no need to seek quality in far away places. There is a unique entrepreneur among us in Turkey which has been invested on by the Silicon Valley in the amount of €2.5 million: Mekanist.net.

Today on Mekanist, which hundreds of thousands of people are able to use thanks to the mobile applications developed for iOS and Android, you can leave comments for places just like on Foursquare, make new friends from this social network and read what people have written about the places you are interested in. Yet, Mekanist has a difference from Foursquare. All the comments you write passes through the approval of editors. That is why I can say that it is more assertive and realistic than Foursquare in terms of content.

Now, let's talk about how to use Yelp or Mekanist. If you are the business manager of a place, do not wait for people to write about you. Include yourself and your circle in the game and start writing and make people write comments about the services you provide. Contribute to the promotion of your website by adding links to your business's website. If you write a beautiful text, your comment could be selected as the comment of the day and shared with everyone on the homepage at the top. In addition, as your comment number increases on Mekanist.net, you are given "Traveler" and "Guru" titles - for now. This way, the comments of new members and the ones of the experienced ones are being evaluated in a different hierarchy.

Mekanist is a social platform on which comments about thousands of businesses are being written and photos are being added by the users themselves. Whether you want it or not, some people write comments about you on here and take photos of your business. All businesses regardless of the sector they are in could benefit from Mekanist.net which is being visited by tens of thousands of people everyday. Thanks to its mobile applications, you can create place cards for the places you've been just like Vedat Milor [29] and you can "check-in" just like on Foursquare.

Maybe, Mekanist which is the Turkish version of USA's Yelp, will merge with Yelp soon. Everything progresses very rapidly these days.

On other location based services and acquisitions

SMS based Dodgeball which was prepared as a dissertation by Foursquare's founders in the year 2000 and considered as the ancestor of Foursquare has been acquired by Google in 2005 and just guess what its name became in 2009. Google Latitude. Although it is not as frequently used as Foursquare, Google Latitude is a service to mark people's exact location on Google Maps using mobile phones, provided that they have a Google account. Right now it is like an "Alien" in incubation stage with the superior Google technology. When you instruct Latitude to follow you, it automatically starts to record the places you go. You never know what the time will show, so you better stay close to Google Latitude.

Turkcell[30] has tried something similar to Foursquare in Turkey with its "Gezenzi" but it was not a successful venture and they had to shut the service down. Turkcell has preferred to continue the game by purchasing a virtual "Badge" from Foursquare instead.

Foursquare's similar competitor Gowalla which started to rise at the same time as Foursquare has been established in 2007 and acquired by Facebook in December 2011. It was shut down 4 months after this acquirement. (March 2012). You may have already noticed. Giants such as Google and Facebook do not like to see strengthening social networks around them. We've started to see similar moves from Twitter as well. They started acquiring services that can become their competitors in the last two years. Well, whom? They have acquired Posterous which has been a rising blog platform, Tweetdeck which was a candidate to decrease Twitter hits and Restengine which was a social marketing automation platform and these are only examples.

The declarations of three giants seem to be oriented towards taking advantage of these firms' strengths and technological infrastructures and integrating these services into their own systems but the truth reveals itself as quite different later on. A trust may be coming our way just like in the case of our GSM operators. I can say that Pinterest's fate would be the thing to make this theory of mine clear.

Oh, and one last thing; Twitter acquired Summify which was an especially favorite service of mine summarizing important events and preventing informational convergence. Upon acquiring, they declared that they wanted to benefit from their know-how and technologies of course and then shut Summify down. If the intentions were good, would they really want to destroy something that they want to befriend?

Anyway, let's proceed.

A FEW EXAMPLES OF NICHE MEDIA

Some services in more niche/vertical areas except the location based ones I've mentioned above and a little better than GPS technology, have started to become popular. Let's talk about the most famous ones of these a little.

GetGlue

GetGlue is a service, in which you can make check-ins just like in Foursquare, earn virtual badges, and it also visually resembles to a game. However, you don't make your check-ins to a place in here. You check-in to a book you've read, to a movie you've watched, to a music you've listened, to a play you've played or to something that crosses your mind. It sound a little absurd at the beginning but there are millions of users of this app as well. In other words, it works. Don't refuse right away by saying "How would it be possible to check-in to a book?" It is possible, pure and simple. I started reading the book of Haruki Murakami named "1Q84" the other day and checked-in to see whether there are others reading this book with more than a thousand pages; I was surprised to see hundreds of comments about it.

You are able to see the ones who checked-in to the book you are reading and the ones who commented on it in the system. Not only are you able to see the comments but you are also able to chat with people over their comments.

In short, GetGlue enables you to see what your friends are watching where, what they are reading and what they are thinking about. It is quite an exciting platform to find people of the same interests and to contact them.

If I were to be a publishing house owner, a film distributor, a game developer or a TV show producer, I would instruct my marketing department to spend all their time in here and send messages to people constantly. There are so many people talking about this on GetGlue that it is impossible for a marketer not to get excited.

Simultaneously 38,000 people have checked-in by saying "I'm Watching the Oscar Ceremony" during 2011 Oscar ceremony for example.

Another difference of GetGlue compared to Foursquare is that you are able to request actual badges in return for the virtual badges you've earned. However, you need to earn 20 badges in total before you can do this.

When you've earned 20 badges, they send you the actual ones free of charge.

GetGlue which was founded in 2008 has become popular in an interesting way and it was not yet acquired by anybody as I was writing these sentences. The coast is clear for marketers on GetGlue my friends. Go for it!

Foodspotting

I was probably one of the first users of this service in Turkey when it made its first appearance. Foodspotting was founded in 2009 by three buddies who asked themselves why it is not possible to write comments only on food while it is possible to check-in and comment on places. This mind matches to my "Harbiyiyorum" thinking very much. If I had the money I would have bought Foodspotting myself. That's how much it corresponds to me.

Foodspotting managed to stand out as a successful social platform amongst many other ventures because it is directly related to foods and not limited to restaurants. The best thing about it is the existence of thousands of cuisines all over the world and millions of dishes in these cuisines. Moreover, you are able to see the real portions regular people are served with and not the exaggerated food photos of the restaurants. In other words, you are able to see what you are going to eat "in full". Not every restaurant has five stars but every place has one or two dishes specific to them. In this sense Foodspotting provides a positive platform enabling you to share your favorite dishes with people. Your followers like, admire and gulp at the photos you share. You have to see the comments written under the photos of food as well. "Yummy, Oh, Boo, Ugh, Yum, My God, etc."

There are virtual badges here as well like Foursquare and GetGlue. However, this time, it is not the Foodspotting team that determines these badges. You are able to prepare your own badges as well. For example, I had prepared a guide for Erzurum cuisine in the year 2011. People who were able to take photos of half of the dishes I've published on my guide and publish these on Foodspotting would earn "Harbiyiyorum Erzurum" badge from me. In other words, I was the one preparing the gift as well as the badge. I was going to treat the ones who were able to take all the photos I've indicated in my guide to a dinner. No one was able to complete the Erzurum tour, the route of which was determined by me, yet. However, I still see tens of people who are using the guide.

You are able to organize a kind of regional food hunt for yourself thanks to the guide service of Foodspotting. And if you are an expert on this, it will be a very correct move to lead people using this kind of guides. There is a guide on Foodspotting, for example, which contains the route of dishes Anthony Bourdain[31] has had during his Istanbul visit. Thousands of people have downloaded this guide in order to use it on their Istanbul visits. Let's suppose you are going to Rome. You can benefit from tens of guides you can find about Rome on Foodspotting.

You, too, can find the guides of such food & beverage authorities (magazines, TVs etc.) on Foodspotting and even prepare your own guide easily if you consider yourself as an authority in this field.

If I were a tourist guide planning to organize a gastronomy tour in Istanbul, I would prepare a Foodspotting guide right away about the best places to eat in Istanbul. I would make this trip more fun by including people in the game in this way. Moreover, hundreds of tourists using the application and planning to come to Istanbul would be able to benefit from my guide. Do you know what this would mean for me? Recognition of course...

A rich couple who are interested in food & beverages may be coming to Istanbul just because of this guide I've created on Foodspotting to taste the delicious dishes of Turkish cuisine and may request my actual guidance for their trip. You never know...

You can create a menu on Foodspotting right away if you own a restaurant. You wouldn't be letting other people to take charge of the photos of your menu by doing so. Or you can take photos of your specialties and gather these together as a guide, and then organize fun promotional events by offering a "dessert" price in return of their photos of these specials every time they come to you. It is possible to design tens of similar campaigns and contests on Foodspotting.

I saw a poster recently in a branch of Sushi-Co announcing that a prize will be given to the people sharing the most creative photos containing a Sushi-Co logo. If I were the marketing executive of Sushi-Co, I wouldn't be hesitating even for a minute to organize this contest on Foodspotting. The number of people who discover sushi on Foodspotting in Turkey is too much to underestimate. Moreover, the users of Foodspotting are people who are exclusively interested in food & beverages.

Today, Foodspotting is downloadable free of charge over all the mobile platforms such as iOS, Android, Blackberry and Windows with the purpose of reaching maximum number of users. Everybody involved in food & beverage business or tourism should without a doubt use this app.

There are millions of food photos shared on Foodspotting all over the world everyday and the number of these photos increases with every passing day.

Snapguide

Have you ever thought of creating "How to?" guides like IKEA does? If you have, here is Snapguide for you.

Snapguide is a service that helps you create visually supported guides in your fields of expertise. For this, you only need an iPhone right now. Later, they would also release its Android version. After you've downloaded the free application on your phone and became a member of the system, you take photos of whatever it is you are preparing a guide about and add supporting and descriptive "How to?" sentences under these photos. Later, the system records this on your behalf and shares it with everybody by opening it for viewing. In this way, thousands of people are able to view your guides from "How to make a stone pizza oven?" to "How to make a candle holder out of an orange?" In addition to viewing, they are also able to comment, add it to their favorites and share it on their own social networks.

How about preparing a guide in your field of expertise?

Couchsurfing

As a hospitality site with more than three millions of members all over the world, Couchsurfing is a platform on which people open their homes to each other and guide each other. People born in nineteen eighty may remember. There were pen pal services before. I had two pen pals; one from Finland, the other from United Kingdom.

Today this need is compensated by the existence of Couchsurfing. Everybody may be a tourist in a foreign country but not everybody may be a Couchsurfer unfortunately. Be prepared for cheap and extraordinary experiences with Couchsurfing which provides a unique platform enabling you to learn local culture of the country you are visiting and to eat like a local there and not like a tourist. There are the new friendships and new perspectives you gain to top it all off.

I shared an article on Pinterest today. I don't know who said it but it is beautiful. There was such a sentence there: "Travel is the only thing that makes you richer amongst all the things you buy."

...and

The number of social ventures in such niche areas is increasing everyday. You are the one to make the final decision about which one would benefit you the most - also by taking your field of expertise into account. However, to tell the truth, the world is becoming more transparent and closer everyday and thanks to that, the transfer of information speeds up incredibly.

It is my duty as a marketing professional to make all the brands I'm interested in present in the relevant niche areas. Many copies appear immediately whenever a social medium has been founded and have become successful. Although this doesn't prevent the first one's success.

Well, which one we should be on?

The leader is the first one. Follow the leader.

SAVANTS AND INTELLECTUALS OF SOCIAL MEDIA

Social media is not only consisted of fun platforms. Wikis and dictionaries also constitute parts of social media. It would be right to talk about them a little as well.

About Wikipedia

Wikipedia is a unique source which became indispensable for us all today as a web-based dictionary everybody can contribute with their knowledge. So much so that it dethroned the most prestigious academic encyclopedia of the world, Britannica. While ten years ago, the newspapers were giving away Britannica and similar encyclopedias for thirty coupons, Wikipedia which was founded in 2001 has become the world's fastest growing and most extensive online encyclopedia with more than 400 millions of individual users daily. Of course this changed the rules of the game fundamentally.

Britannica, which was being printed since 1768, announced that it won't be coming out in printed format as of 2010 (the end of an era.) So, 200 years of tradition has begun to take a completely different direction with the Internet. Despite Britannica's declaration indicating that it will exist on online media as of that date, now, Wikipedia will be the first to come to mind when the subject is Internet encyclopedia. I feel sorry for Britannica but they were probably unaware of their becoming a part of the history while they were busy with the history in such a detailed way. The news of their going down in history was announced by Wikipedia first. Currently, while Wikipedia offers free content, Britannica's insistence on paid content is a pathetic condition for them. If I were in Britannica's place, I wouldn't be giving up my printed version even at the expense of decrease in my sales. I wouldn't ever go online. I would carry on the tradition more or less by doing so.

The age for encyclopedias is now the age of Wikipedia and Wikipedia functions according to the logic of Web 2.0. Yes, there still are editors, controllers, historians and experts but history is not written by a committee anymore as it was with printed encyclopedias. People of all ages are able to contribute to Wikipedia by adding information and editing texts written under the titles as long as these conform to the rules and the format. Any of us is able to do this. Just go on and try. It is enough for that text to be objective and really adding some value to that title for the approval. Moreover, you don't even need to be a member. If you spend some time on Wikipedia, it would be very easy for you to learn how to edit those texts. You will see "Edit" links under the titles on every page. You are able to intervene in the text the moment you click on this link. Of course this doesn't mean that everything you will write will be approved immediately. Your text passes through an evaluation conducted by a high committee and relevant experts and then takes its place within the limitless mine of information of Wikipedia permanently.

Whatever you would be searching for in the name of information on the Internet, you would find a Wikipedia result about it.

You should necessarily take action in order for your corporation, brand or yourself if you are an artist to be present on Wikipedia. Wikipedia is a pretty prestigious place. It is serious. It is academic. Wikipedia is an encyclopedia everybody in the world writes collectively! So it is really exciting.

About Quora

Two Facebook employees who got sick of chattiness of Facebook founded Quora in 2009. Although many of the entrepreneurs have developed services for fun on social networks, their main starting point was the lack of an actual social platform for serious texts.

Quora is actually a kind of Q&A application. You can see a question such as "Where the best is place n Istanbul?" as well as "What is the thing that makes an object and art work?" on here... However, you can find answers for all kind of questions here and you can also contribute if you like with your own answers to these questions.

Let's take a look at some of the questions.

"Which food is the one you cannot say no to?"

"What are the fundamental differences between Aristotle's and Plato's ethical philosophies?"

"Why is Facebook obliged to develop high quality software?"

"Why did Twitter change its bird logo?"

"Why is Pinterest so successful?"

These questions and alike, are only a few of tens of thousands of question titles. Questions are also divided into categories within themselves. The best questions and the best titles are discussed in a different place.

In short, if you have questions to ask about your field of expertise or things to say about your hobbies, Quora is just the right place for you. Moreover, if you are fed up with the frivolity of Facebook and Twitter, this place is pretty serious. Quora is a website with a more academic inclination just like Wikipedia. That is why, please be aware that your answers could not contain smileys etc.

Contribute to Quora in your fields of expertise with questions you can answer. Quora is one of the most important showcases on which you can show your expertise.

SOCIAL BOOKMARKINGS

You would generally tag the posts you write on blogs. This is something to facilitate the categorization in your blog whenever you write about someone. Tagging is also a facility for search engines. The follower of your blog could easily read the texts under the subjects with similar tags thanks to tagging. Let's suppose that you are writing about an iOS application. Then your probable text tags would be: "iOS, Apple, iPhone, iPad and mobile software".

Social bookmarkings are just like the generic and communal versions of the tagging you are doing on your own blogs. The platforms on which everybody is sharing the links of their writings cumulatively are called social bookmarkings.

Let's explain a little more. Think of a blog. You add all the link addresses of everybody's writings to this blog and tag each link with a related word. This blog starts to draw attention of the people who are interested in similar tags since it has the links from everybody. The link you share gets ratings from the users. This way, you convey your message to more people.

We've shared our content on main social media (Facebook, Twitter, Pinterest, Youtube) but we want to provide traffic from more sources. What should we do? We will use social bookmarkings of course.

Started in 2003 with Delicious.com, these services which are grounded on tagging and sharing links, and which facilitate finding related texts and shares for people just as bookmarks continue to exist today under the leadership of Stumbleupon, Digg, Reddit and Newsvine.

Although they may majorly seem like services to optimize search engines (by providing backlink to your website), you should remember that your shares are being followed by various broadcasting corporations through these channels. If we are in the business of digital marketing and we have included social boookmarkings in our strategy, we have to use them. At the end, we want our message to reach as many people as possible. Don't we? So, open accounts on Delicious, Digg and Reddit right away.

CLEAN SOCIAL MEDIA

Google +
Yes, you've heard it right: clean social media.

It seems pretty normal to me that the follower numbers in Facebook and Twitter keep on inflating as long as the marketing executives of the firms are motivated to impress their CEOs with numbers. Everybody knows now that at least half of the people who have tens of thousands of millions (!) of followers on Twitter actually have fake followers. This is true for Facebook pages of the firms as well. Well, "fine feathers make fine birds" is a saying that scores points in every period after all.

Of course, we can discuss more on whether quality or quantity should be preferred. However, I had the chance to get to know Google + better while I was writing this book and it made me forget all the social media algorithms I knew to this day. I was even intoxicated by it.

I will have just one question for the ones who think that Google + is nothing, that it cannot compete with Facebook, that it doesn't even have active users. Do you have a Gmail account? If you do, you've already started to use Google +. Just that you don't know about it yet.

I've mentioned in previous chapters of the book that Google is more like our Pythagoras acting on logic and mathematical archetypes. I was not wrong in this theory. Google has very large wheels and that is why they turn very slowly but Google moves in a very confident way in terms of "Social Search".

During the interview I've made with Aslihan Ulutas, the Individual Product Marketing Manager of Google Turkey, I learned that Google + is not a product competing with Facebook and that it is known as a project directed at Web 3.0

(or whatever the name will be) infrastructure in which some of the tried Google products are being re-experienced. She called Google + as "Google Plus Project" during the whole interview.

When the interview was over, things have already started to fall into place in my mind. Google was actually bringing together all the services it has produced until today (whether actually understood and used or not, e.g. Google Wave) in Google + for the superior "Social Google" experience of the future. For example, if you use the product of "Contact" on your Gmail, you will encounter its similar as "Circles" on Google +. You see Google Calendar feature on Google + under the "Events" title in a more improved way. If you use Google Docs, this experience turns into a different experience with video calls and ability to work together with ten people on your files in Google +'s "Hangouts". Picasa has also been transformed into something else in Google + with your mobile device. Furthermore, I learned that all the content we've tagged as +1 will be filtered in two separate results in the coming days when we make Google searches: 1. The related content +1'ed by the people in our circle, 2. The classical and organic results Google is providing us with related to the words we search for.

Here are the baby steps of "Social Search"!

Well, why do I call Google + as clean social media? On the contrary of other social media accounts, Google + allows you to share your content according to the circles you've created (friends, family, business, food & beverages, my students, the ones I follow etc.). This way, I am able to share photos I took with my wife and kids only with my family and to make the content I will share as course content available only to my students. In other words, I am able to prevent information pollution by avoiding pumping all my posts to all the people who follow me.

I participated in the Google + Workshop the following day of the interview I made with Aslihan Ulutas. This way, I've seen the Google + services' superior features compared to other social networks with the help of the integration of many interactive services; these services were ranging from "Hangout" product which provided 10 people to make conference calls simultaneously with the opportunity to make changes on the documents they were working on to "Event" product which enabled collecting all the photos and shares of the people who have participated in the same event in the same pool.

Moreover, corporate/individual pages you create on Google + are being approved by Google center's editors. In other words, your followers could not be mistaken even if others create a page on your behalf or in the name of your corporation since these wouldn't be "Verified Accounts". Indeed, Google + is proceeding with confidence by offering superior services but also silently and subtly, just like the way Gmail entered our lives.

Google eliminated other search engines for starters. Later, their Chrome and Gmail products dethroned Hotmail and Explorer. Google + is marching like a German tank with its superior Google experience and its vision of shaping the Internet of the future. Hold tight!

CHAPTER 3

The Road Map

MOBILE APPLICATIONS AND MARKETING COMMUNICATION

I won't be talking with numbers. This is a fact like the sudden entrance of cell phones to our lives. Everybody will own a smart phone one day. It makes no difference whether it has iOS operating system, Android, or Windows. People are going to surf on Internet with the computer-phones they hand in their hands. This process has already started. Just watch the next ten years.

Today, many ventures have already designed their business plans according to mobile phones and their numbers are increasing everyday. Some of the leading social services I've mentioned in this book (Foursquare, GetGlue, Snapguide) exist only on mobile devices.

In the coming years, many mobile applications for every brand and product will become parts of the digital marketing communication activities just as Facebook or Twitter is today.

Smart phones and the applications developed for them came with the concept of "Utility Marketing". In other words, corporations will no longer be satisfied with the mobile versions of their websites. They will go beyond this and try to develop applications that won't bring them direct sales but instead, offer them the opportunity of indirect marketing by benefitting the clients or potential customers just as it is in the nature of social media itself. There are already examples of this.

If you are an architecture office, for example, you will develop a measuring application which carries the interface of your corporation. If you are a creative agency, you will develop an application named "iAnnemi Aramadim - ididntCallMyMother". These will be downloaded on thousands of mobile phones and consumers will always be in interaction with your brand in this way.

Nike has already started to provide a service with its "Nike +" app which doesn't relate directly to the product it is selling but which could be used by everyone who works out. This app measures your performance of trekking or running, compares it with your later tracks and whispers to the subconscious of the user saying "NIKE" every time it comes to sports and running.

I hope you have understood what I mean by grasping the importance of mobile apps.

As I constantly told in this book, the process is now about the efforts you spend in order to be the first to come to the minds of people when they need you rather than direct marketing and that is why you should try to make your product or service visible in places where the most people are. Smart phones have also become important parts of marketing communications now. I would recommend you to read an article of mine I've written on SMN if you would like to learn more about "Utility Marketing".

WHERE SHOULD WE FOLLOW THE DAY'S AGENDA?

There are many sources I follow. I listed the ones I follow

the most below. These sources would feed and satisfy everybody who is interested in social media.
- Thenextweb.com
- Techcrunch.com
- Socialbakers.com
- Mashable.com
- Lifehacker.com
- Readwriteweb.com
- Geeksugar.com
- Netted.net

WHO IS THIS SOCIAL MEDIA EXPERT?

I have given a speech on this title last year in a seminar.

I serve as a social media consultant to corporations from various sectors about two years. During this whole time, I interviewed tens of candidates who applied for a job in our firm. Today, you encounter thousands of social media experts when you make a search on Linkedin. Everybody comes to saying "I'm an expert". Some of them brag about their follower numbers on Twitter while some think that using Facebook and Twitter would be enough to conduct a brand's social media marketing strategies. There are also others who request an interview with you with a cover letter that says "I use Facebook more than 10 years". Oh yeah?!

More than half of the people I gave an appointment to meet were not able to find our office. (We are at a central place, on a main street.) And some of them notified me that they will not be coming at the last minute by writing a message to me over Facebook even though I had included my mobile phone number in my invite e-mail.

We ask ourselves together with my partners: "How would these guys conduct the marketing communications of our clients when they are not even able to communicate correctly for themselves?"

The grass looks greener on the other side of the fence. I ask the ones who come: "Do you have a blog?" I don't even give a chance anyway to the ones answering with "No". Still, I say "Come and start" to the ones who do not look like know-it-alls and who are open to learning. But this time, these people loose their minds since the grass is not that green on this side. Other agencies in the sector are probably experiencing these processes I mention as well.

For a whole year, I looked for a person who is willing about learning the social media, who has strong communication skills, who is responsible and open to learning, and who writes on a blog. However I couldn't find anybody and gave up searching somebody who can work in this area in Istanbul.

I had given a social media training entitled "Stars of the East" to young and entrepreneur people of Erzurum in 2011. The project was funded by European Union and it was a series of trainings entitled "Entrepreneurship Trainings" given to 44 college students from Erzurum with the aim of putting forth the valuable assets of East using Internet ventures.

I still conduct works of social media and digital marketing strategies of brands together with two active female students I have trained in this series. On top of it, they are in Erzurum. And I am in Istanbul. Yet, I don't worry at all.

I would like to correct a misunderstanding. I've named this chapter as "Who is this social media expert?" due to the popularity of the concept of social media today. However, there is no such thing as social media expert. There are "marketing communication experts". And that is really hard to find these days.

The person who is interested in social media has to know how all the services I've mentioned in this book work and what they are.

He/she must follow newly released services and ventures, and must learn what kind of changes are happening in this field before anybody else. He/she must have a blog and must also know how to fill it. Be careful, I didn't say that he/she must write on a blog. However, he/she should know how the blog functions, how it is kept, how the content is provided, how the traffic is created, in other words he/she should know which functions a blog has in terms of marketing communications. He/she should understand the interrelations of social media platforms very well and be able to predict how to use which platform. The social media expert should be happy of the results that come out when he/she "Googles" his/her name. The results that come on the first page when he/she searches his/her own name should be information related to him/her. Social media expert should be able to think as a marketer and act as a publisher. He/she has to have precise information about how the ads on social networks function and how they are used. Additionally, the readers of this book are also expected to be social media experts.

THE ROAD MAP

Actually, all the titles of this book contain factors that can be considered as a guide when a product/service or corporation is determining their own marketing plan on social media. Every corporation which adapts these titles to itself while determining its social media plan would be creating its own social media road map.

This book is a road map for everybody regardless of their being corporations or individuals. The only thing you need to do for this is to get a pen and a paper and write down the titles found in here as a list, and then determine what you can do about your own brand from the inspiration you get from what I have said under every title. I know that it requires a hard work even to fill all these titles up. However, you need to do this. I put forth the most functional ones amongst hundreds of social media platforms when I was writing this book.

It would be enough for you to define action plans for every title according to the way you want to exist on social media. Some of them may not be suitable to you, so just cross them out. Some of the social media platforms may change in time but nevertheless, every platform would have similar marketing processes conforming to its own discourse.

If we were to summarize this book, we would say:

You'll be sincere. You'll produce high quality content. You'll create content that is worth marketing and talking about. Later, you'll share your content primarily on the main drags (Facebook, Twitter). You'll support these posts with ads on social media according to your target group and your budget. You'll make your posts reach more people by making use of "Social Bookmarkings". You won't be negligent to Twitter Search. This way, you'll be able to form closer relationships with people by one-to-one contacts. You'll produce videos and presentations about your passion and your field of expertise. You'll take photos. You'll continue to share these firstly on social video, image and presentation sharing sites and then again on the main drags. You'll try to understand your Facebook community and be in a constant communication with them. You'll use the ads again in order to increase the number of likes of your group. You'll keep your group active but without pushing them too much. You'll find niche social media platforms related to your field and increase your activities on these vertical platforms. You'll be spending time with a more correct minority related to the product or service you are offering by doing so. You'll constant listen and communicate. You'll follow the innovations that will benefit you the most and if necessary, include new platforms in your social media plans as well.

Today, the invisible wall between social media and the Internet has been pulled down. Now, social media is not an innovation related only to marketing or public relation activities of a company. It relates to the whole of a corporation's strategy. Smart managers have already grasped this fact. Here, there should be no talk of money. The principal capital consists of participation, value creating interaction and to create value in relationships. The ones who correctly invest in this capital will increase their profitability.

Regardless of the size of a corporation, its success passes through the correct usage of social media. Social media is a reality acting on all the units of a corporation. Customer relations, sales, after sales services, HR, IT, whatever else there is...

Social media has changed the rules of the game. TV ads worth millions of liras are not the main factor to trigger purchasing behavior anymore. You may have noticed that corporations are leading people to their Facebook or Twitter pages now even on their TV commercials. The winners of the future are the ones who trigger innovation in their products by providing superior services on social media.

You should set your target as follows: When someone searches for your product or services on Google, they should first encounter you in text, video, image or music formats. Too much work is required for all this to happen. Work, work, work. For social media is a demanding job.

THE BLINDNESS TO CHANGE, DETERMINING CORRECT SOCIAL MEDIA PLATFORMS FOR THE BRANDS AND THE FUTURE

Now, let's look a little at the boom part of the job.

A friend of mine shared something that surprised me recently on Facebook. Over five hundred thousand social media platforms have sprouted up in the last ten years. This means five hundred thousand hopeful investments and jobs coming right after Web 2.0 with logos resembling to candies. All of this may sound pretty good from the above perspective.

Yet I will ask: Could the life of anyone be enough to get to know that much services? Let's say we lived long enough. Will we be living just for these?

In his book named "The Naked Ape", the famous anthropologist Desmond Morris suggests that a human being could have only one hundred or, in the case of being too much social, maximum one hundred and fifty people with whom he/she can have a healthy communication at the moment of living.

I have more than a thousand friends on Facebook for instance. Many of them are people who added me from my speeches and seminars. They have added me and it stayed that way. We have never asked how each other is doing or sent a message. However, the number of my relatives, friends, people in my business circle and people with whom we mutually ask about each other doesn't actually exceed 150. Healthy relationship means reciprocal communication. It should create a benefit for both parties.

People used to flow in the sites with .com (dot com) extensions in the early days of 2000s as if they were on a raid for gold. Many Internet brand have risen during that period but many have sunk into oblivion too. In those days, Google was not the first thing to come to mind when the subject was search engines and there were many services claiming to register our websites to hundreds of search engines if we paid a certain fee. Just for this reason, we used to think that registration to a search engine is a paid service. Actually, we observe that nothing much changed at least about these kinds of methods to make money since those days. Nowadays, the loot happens like this: Various intermediary corporations claim to secure your name/brand on hundreds of popular social media sites; of course, in exchange for a certain fee. If there are five hundred thousand social media platforms as we've indicated above as of this moment, the most optimistic guess would be that at least 300 hundred of these are necessarily popular, wouldn't it?

So, these intermediaries reserve your brand's or corporation's name on these "supposedly popular" social media sites on your behalf. Yet the main question is this: How are we supposed to know which of these would benefit us amongst all those platforms and such a rapid change? As I've indicated before, even the experts weren't able to see the rising popularity of Pinterest which is glorified today.

Then, what we should do is actually pretty simple: We'll spend all our energy on the social media platforms which are the most popular ones of today by preferring the ones we like to use the most. There is no need to burn out our brains while trying to use all of them at once. Later, we may not be able to use any of them at all god forbid!

Additionally, all of the media I've mentioned in this book are the ones I've personally tested and approved and you will benefit a lot if you manage to use only these platforms correctly. If there is anyone who has more than twenty services for a brand, they should Tweet me. I'll come to inspect.

If I asked you to list the top two social media sites you can think of, most of you would answer me with Facebook and Twitter since human brain is related to brand perception. Therefore, this comes to mean: Fingers point to Facebook and Twitter and you should do justice to these places. Every plus you will put on top of these will be recorded as brownie points on your behalf.

Social media is a tool of marketing communications and the tools can change in time. You may have already noticed this. The majority of the services I've talked about in this book are inventions of the last five years. And many of them have been sold to another one in the last three years. In other words, Mekanist could become Yelp Turkey in the near future. And Yelp.com could become Yelp Google. As a matter of fact, right now, the whole world is after new ventures in such a way that could be acquired by Facebook, Google and Twitter. And the investors hesitate in supporting the entrepreneurs who do not aim for this anyway.

I can't help saying this as well: The initial investment amount of a successful business venture is five hundred thousand dollars. Nobody should dream about establishing their own Facebook and Twitter with forty or fifty thousand dollars. (I hope to benefit the entrepreneurs in the start-up world with this bit.) People start to make plans of successful "Exits" at the moment they see the projects. This is the entrepreneurial model of today.

In future Facebook may be replaced by Grasbook or Twitter by Dwizzer. Regardless of the future names of social media platforms mentioned herein, it is certain that we will be encountering them as new services to contribute more to people's communications. The most important indicator at this point for a marketing professional to decide on the correct social media platform to be on, is the intuition of where people are looking at and what they are listening to. I take the manifesto of "money is where the people are" a step further and say "money is where the people are looking at, what they are listening to." Today, people listen to social media channels just as TVs and radios of old days and look at their mobile phones all day. The world is changing with a rapid pace. Additionally, the change is happening faster and faster everyday.

Before, we had more time and fewer options to spend our money on. Now, we all have little time and many options to spend our money on.

Even though we know all that, there will be trade as long as there are people on the world and there will be marketing as long as there is trade. We will be seeking marketers' help in order to find the product we need although we have many options before us. That is why we need smart marketing professionals who have analyzed the grounds of digital processes thoroughly.

Americans have an idiom that says "jumped to shark". We can call it as "taking a nosedive". It means the sudden becoming meaningless of something while everything was going smooth up until that point, loosing its meaning after a point... The example sense could be found in Quentin Tarantino's movie From Dusk Till Dawn.

The movie goes on in a classical, adventurous atmosphere for the first hour, and then everybody gets shocked with an "Oh my!" effect created by the unexpected and sudden transformation of everybody in the bar into zombies.

We will, of course, experience this on social media as well. As a matter of fact, we have already started to see it. We've laughed a lot to the line of "Facebook is flooded with hobos" in the movie Recep Ivedik. Don't you think that the environment has already become very messy even though it is not flooded with hobos?

I still believe that all these nosedives will be laden with new productions and new developments. It is in human nature to learn lessons and to always try to make something better than before.

I've heard it from Gulsen Caltil, the owner of Ekol Drama: "Water always flows forward." Let an aphorism concerning this subject come from Aristotle as well: "Every art and every inquiry, and similarly every action and pursuit, is thought to aim at some good."

HIGGS BOSON AND SOCIAL MEDIA

Are "new players" or "changing players" on social media a big deal? When electrons in the atom were discovered in 1897, people were still plating seeds on the fields, postmen on horses were carrying the posts and everybody was minding their own business in their daily lives.

This discovery didn't mean much to anybody in those days. There were a lot of people who were saying "what does it have to do with us?" Yet, not even a day passes without the use of electrons in today's technology. All the inventions such as TV, telephone, radio, computer etc. are technologies related to the discovery of electrons and their interpretations.

One of the most important scientific discoveries of the history was made recently during the experiment conducted within the "Large Hadron Collider" at CERN/Switzerland. Two protons were collided with one another in an emptier and colder environment than space during this experiment which is at the extremes in everything. An energy thousands of times more than that of the temperature of sun's core came out as a result of the experiment. The purpose was to prove the existence of subatomic particle called Higgs Boson and scientists have managed to see the Higgs Boson where they estimated it would be at the end of this experiment. In other words, they did it! What a joy for scientists! This appeared in our press too as much as it should appear: 1 day. At the end, Higgs Boson is not much different than the electron found in 1897. Right now, nobody is certain about what Higgs Boson could do.

Let me try to explain further. Higgs Boson is the most

important subatomic particle that gives the matter its mass. Human beings would understand how matter gets its mass by understanding this subatomic particle. So, what does this mean? This means that human beings will be able to create matter in the universe out of nothing in the coming years.

We can say that Higgs Boson is the subatomic particle just as our DNA that has the information of the substance of the matter and that is in spin-0 at a projection which is completely in control of the matter's ideal data and that it gives the matter its mass. (What a definition! I made it.)

Why do I talk about this? First of all, technological advancements go on with a stunning speed today and the results of today are becoming the beginnings of tomorrow. That is why it doesn't matter if there is Facebook today and another medium tomorrow. The important thing is the position and experience this technology has brought for the whole of humanity in digital marketing communications.

Secondly, we can also identify this in the same way with the archetype unique to every brand. Here, there is a need for marketing professionals who can replace the Higgs Boson conceptually and determine the real values of the brands. In other words, it is very important to find people who are masters of their domain in marketing communications and social media and who can analyze the real grounds a brand is founded upon in a correct way. When you find these people, your concerns about what medium you are on or how you should use these media will not matter at all.

They will always keep the projection right about your product, service or brand; just like the Higgs Boson.

/ Kadikoy, Istanbul, July 2012

KEEP IN TOUCH

You can always reach me @
salihseckin@gmail.com
http://salihseckinsevinc.com
http://twitter.com/Temurah
http://facebook.com/yazarsalihseckin
http://www.linkedin.com/in/salihseckinsevinc
http://about.me/salihseckinsevinc

ENDNOTES

1 A famous ice-cream master in Istanbul.
2 Turkish contemporary artist/painter. For more information http://peyamigurel.com
3 Optimist Books, A leading publishing company in Turkey. Focused on publishing business books.
4 Author's food blog. http://harbiyiyorum.com
5 A city located in north-east side of Turkey. Known as Mecca of Kebabs. It is also called as "Antep"
6 A famous gourmet of Turkey.
7 The famous kebab restaurant in Gaziantep.
8 A special meatball restaurant in Kadikoy, Istanbul. They are making special meatballs of Inegol, Bursa
9 A tripe soup restaurant in Beyoglu district, Istanbul, Turkey
10 One of the best Katmer master in Gaziantep, Turkey
11 Gourmet
12 A national newspaper of Turkey
13 Turkish Lira
14 Movie, get more details from: http://www.imdb.com/title/tt1285309/

[15] Surfer's heaven. A beach with powerful winds. Cesme, Izmir, Turkey.

[16] For more information: http://en.wikipedia.org/wiki/WikiLeaks

[17] But now, Wordpress again! as of 22.01.2014

[18] http://techcrunch.com

[19] http://sosyalmedyanedir.net

[20] http://bikafalar.com

[21] http://myspace.com

[22] A Sufi Mystic - For more information, please visit http://en.wikipedia.org/wiki/Rumi

[23] Internet Relay Chat, created in 1995 - For more info please visit - http://en.wikipedia.org/wiki/MIRC

[24] A city in east side of Turkey

[25] http://www.youtube.com/watch?v=ohfIC7AF-AY

[26] http://canvastar.com

[27] App Store Link of Text Here - https://itunes.apple.com/app/text-here-create-funny-pictures/id532506770

[28] A famous street in Beyoglu district, Istanbul

[29] A famous gourmet in Turkey

[30] Turkish GSM company

[31] Gourmet, Traveller